FRUIT OF THE SPIRIT

WISDOM FROM THE APOSTOLIC FATHERS

EDITED BY

GEORGE D. ZGOURIDES, PSY.D.

Dear Bill,

Best wishes in the New Year.

Love,

Ant & Erin 2007

ISBN 1-928653-13-8

REGINA ORTHODOX PRESS
P.O. Box 5288
Salisbury, MA 01952
800-636-2470
Non-U.S.A. 978-463-0730
www.reginaorthodoxpress.com

Contents

Introduction

"But the fruit of the Spirit is love, joy, peace, longsuffering, kindness, goodness, faithfulness, gentleness, self-control. Against such there is no law." (Galatians 5:22)

"For you were once darkness, but now you are light in the Lord. Walk as children of light (for the fruit of the Spirit is in all goodness, righteousness, and truth), finding out what is acceptable to the Lord." (Ephesians 5:8-10)

This book began as a resource for my personal use. Over the years, I have often desired a handy list of quotations from the early Patristic period on a variety of theological topics. In particular, I have become interested in the writings of various Christian authors of the first and second centuries—the so-called Apostolic Fathers. The most notable of these writers are Clement of Rome, Polycarp, Ignatius of Antioch, Barnabas, Justin Martyr, Irenaeus, Athenagoras, and Clement of Alexandria, as well as some other lesser-known individuals. While the sayings collected for this volume are in no way meant to be exhaustive, I believe they offer some feel for these Apostolic Fathers' perspectives on the developing Christian faith of their day.

For this small book, I have chosen as my theme Paul's texts on the "fruit" of the Holy Spirit. In the following pages, you will find some of the very early Father's most thought-provoking and inspiring comments on various Christian qualities as described in the New Testament.

Of course, I make no claims regarding the genuineness or authenticity of any of these texts, nor do I presume to have insight into any of these authors' original intent or context, ecclesiastical authority, theological inclination, or commitment to the Historic Church. Instead, I invite you, the reader, to draw your own conclusions about these writings, as well as apply the ones you believe will prove of spiritual benefit in your walk with Christ.

– George D. Zgourides, Editor

A Note on the Authors

The average reader knows little about the lives of the Apostolic Fathers. This is understandable given the antiquity of these authors, not to mention the fact their writings have not been widely available in modern times. While extensive commentary is beyond the scope of this book, a very brief word on several of the best-known Apostolic Fathers is in order.

CLEMENT OF ROME (fl. c. 96) was an early Bishop of Rome and probably the third successor to Peter. While two letters, or epistles, to the Corinthians are credited to Clement, the first is widely considered to be genuine and his primary claim to fame. The second, the actual authorship of which remains unknown, is often said to be the earliest surviving Christian sermon.

POLYCARP (traditionally c. 69-c. 155) was Bishop of Smyrna and a leading figure in preserving Christianity against such groups as the Marcionites and the Docetists.

IGNATIUS OF ANTIOCH (c. 35-c. 107) was Bishop of Antioch in Syria and wrote extensively on Christology, the Eucharist, and the importance of being in communion with the bishop as the best protection against heresy and error. His letters give the first evidence of the three-tiered clerical model in use today—that of bishops, presbyters, and deacons.

BARNABAS (dates unknown) was one of Paul's fellow missionaries and, as tradition holds, was the founder of the Cypriot Church.

JUSTIN MARTYR (c.100-c.165), the author of numerous early Church documents, was especially concerned with reconciling faith with reason. His writings, including the First Apology, are a valuable witness to the liturgical beliefs and practices of his time.

IRENAEUS (c. 130-c. 200) was possibly a native of Smyrna, though few details of his life are known. Of his two works that have survived, Against the Heresies is a classic criticism of early Gnostic systems.

ATHENAGORAS (2nd cent.) was a Christian apologist and philosopher from Athens. He was one of the first theologians to outline an extensive philosophical defense of the Christian doctrine of God as Three in One.

CLEMENT OF ALEXANDRIA (c. 150-c. 215), a theologian, became the head of the Catechetical School at Alexandria, which taught various associations between the Christian faith and Greek culture (including the Platonic philosophical tradition). Clement of Alexandria regarded Greek philosophy as a Divine gift that could also be used in the pursuit of Christian perfection.

A Note on the Texts

The presented texts and translations used in this book were collected and adapted from the standard editions and translations of Arthur Cleveland Coxe (1818-1896), William Wake (1657-1737), William Hone (1780-1842), and Jeremiah Jones (1693-1724). Every effort was made to retain the translators' original sentence structure, capitalization, and punctuation, except where changes were necessary for clarity. Biblical verses were taken from the New King James Version.

The author wishes to express his thanks to Christie Zgourides and Genie Schaeffer for their editorial assistance, and Dr. Frank A. Schaeffer for his expert guidance.

Chapter One

LOVE

λοϖε

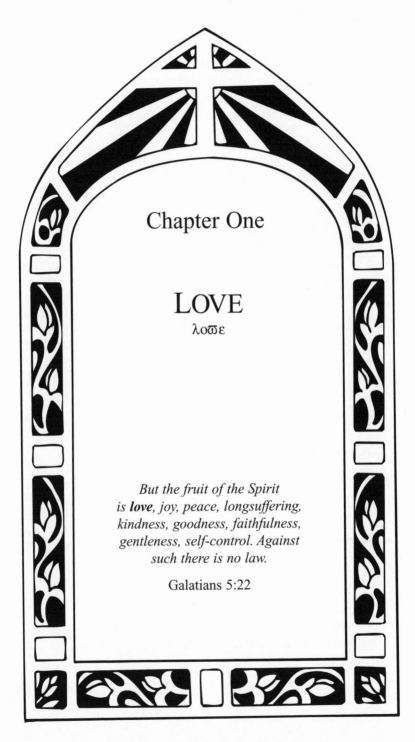

But the fruit of the Spirit
*is **love**, joy, peace, longsuffering,*
kindness, goodness, faithfulness,
gentleness, self-control. Against
such there is no law.

Galatians 5:22

Clement of Rome

First Epistle to the Corinthians

LET us then draw near to Him with holiness of spirit, lifting up pure and undefiled hands unto Him, loving our gracious and merciful Father, who has made us partakers in the blessings of His elect. – *Chapter 29*

THE height to which love exalts is unspeakable. Love unites us to God. Love covers a multitude of sins. Love beareth all things, is longsuffering in all things. There is nothing base, nothing arrogant in love. Love admits of no schisms: love gives rise to no seditions: love does all things in harmony. By love have all the elect of God been made perfect; without love nothing is well-pleasing to God. In love has the Lord taken us to Himself. On account of the Love he bore us, Jesus Christ our Lord gave His blood for us by the will of God; His flesh for our flesh, and His soul for our souls. – *Chapter 49*

YE see, beloved, how great and wonderful a thing is love, and that there is no declaring its perfection. Who is fit to be found in it, except such as God has vouchsafed to render so? Let us pray, therefore, and implore of His mercy, that we may live blameless in love, free from all human partialities for one above another. – *Chapter 50*

BLESSED are we, beloved, if we keep the commandments of God in the harmony of love; that so through love our sins may be forgiven us. – *Chapter 50*

FOR such as live in fear and love would rather that they themselves than their neighbors should be involved in suffering. – *Chapter 51*

Mathetes

Epistle to Diognetus

THE soul loves the flesh that hates it, and loves also the members; Christians likewise love those that hate them. – *Chapter 6*

AND if you love Him, you will be an imitator of His kindness. And do not wonder that a man may become an imitator of God. He can, if he is willing. – *Chapter 10*

Polycarp

Epistle to the Philippians

HE THAT hath love is far from all sin. – *Chapter 3*

Ignatius

Epistle to the Ephesians

BUT inasmuch as love suffers me not to be silent in regard to you, I have therefore taken upon me first to exhort you that ye would all run together in accordance with the will of God. – *Chapter 3*

THEREFORE in your concord and harmonious love, Jesus Christ is sung. – *Chapter 4*

FOR let us either fear the wrath to come, or let us love the present joy in the life that now is; and let our present and true joy be only this, to be found in Christ Jesus, that we may truly live. – *Chapter 11*

FOR the beginning is faith, and the end is love. Now these two, being inseparably connected together, are of God, while all other things which are requisite for a holy life follow after them. – *Chapter 14*

NO man making a profession of faith ought to sin, nor one possessed of love to hate his brother. – *Chapter 14*

STAND fast, brethren, in the faith of Jesus Christ, and in His love, in His passion, and in His resurrection. – *Chapter 20*

Epistle to the Magnesians

LET us all therefore love one another in harmony, and let no one look upon his neighbor according to the flesh, but in Christ Jesus. – *Chapter 6*

Epistle to the Trallians

AND do ye, every man, love one another with an undivided heart. – *Chapter 13*

Epistle to the Romans

I DESIRE the bread of God, the heavenly bread, the bread of life, which is the flesh of Jesus Christ, the Son of God, who became afterwards of the seed of David and Abraham; and I desire the drink, namely His blood, which is incorruptible love and eternal life. – *Chapter 7*

Epistle to the Philadelphians

WHEREFORE I write boldly to your love, which is worthy of God, and exhort you to have but one faith, and one kind of preaching, and one Eucharist. – *Chapter 4*

HUSBANDS, love your wives, as fellow-servants of God, as your own body, as the partners of your life, and your coadjutors in the procreation of children. – *Chapter 4*

DO nothing without the bishop; keep your bodies as the temples of God; love unity; avoid divisions; be ye followers of Paul, and of the rest of the apostles, even as they also were of Christ. – *Chapter 7*

Epistle to the Smyrnaeans

LET not high place puff any one up: for that which is worth all is faith and love, to which nothing is to be preferred. – *Chapter 6*

FOR the chief points are faith towards God, hope towards Christ, the enjoyment of those good things for which we look, and love towards God and our neighbor. – *Chapter 6*

Epistle to Polycarp

SPEAK to my sisters, that they love the Lord, and be satisfied with their husbands both in the flesh and spirit. In like manner also, exhort my brethren, in the name of Jesus Christ, that they love their wives, even as the Lord the Church. – *Chapter 5*

Let your baptism endure as your arms; your faith as your helmet; your love as your spear; your patience as a complete panoply. – *Chapter 6*

Second Epistle to the Ephesians

AND ye are prepared for the building of God the Father, and raised up on high by the instrument of Jesus Christ, which is the cross; and ye are drawn by the rope, which is the Holy Spirit; and your pulley is your faith, and your love is the way which leadeth up on high to God. – *Chapter 9*

Epistle to the Tarsians

YE husbands, love your wives; and ye wives, your husbands. Ye children, reverence your parents. – *Chapter 9*

Epistle to the Antiochians

LET the husbands love their wives, remembering that, at the creation, one woman, and not many, was given to one man. – *Chapter 9*

Epistle to the Deacon Hero of Antioch

IT is fitting, therefore, to love those that were the authors of our birth (but only in the Lord), inasmuch as a man can produce no children without a woman. It is right, therefore, that we should honor those who have had a part in giving us birth. – *Chapter 4*

EXHORT my sisters to love God, and be content with their own husbands only. In like manner, exhort my brethren also to be content with their own wives. – *Chapter 5*

Epistle to the Philippians

LOVE one another in the Lord, as being the images of God. Take heed, ye husbands, that ye love your wives as your own members. Ye wives also, love your husbands, as being one with them in virtue of your union. – *Chapter 13*

Barnabas

Epistle

EVERY word which proceedeth out of your mouth in faith and love shall tend to bring conversion and hope to many. – *Chapter 11*

THOU shalt love Him that created thee; thou shalt glorify Him that redeemed thee from death. Thou shalt be simple in heart, and rich in spirit. – *Chapter 19*

THOU shalt love thy neighbor more than thine own soul. – *Chapter 19*

THOU shalt love, as the apple of thine eye, every one that speaketh to thee the word of the Lord. – *Chapter 19*

Justin Martyr

First Apology

REASON directs those who are truly pious and philosophical to honor and love only what is true, declining to follow traditional opinions, if these be worthless. – *Chapter 2*

On the Resurrection

WHEREFORE the Savior also taught us to love our enemies, since, says He, what thank have ye? So that He has shown us that it is a good work not only to love those that are begotten of Him, but also those that are without. And what He enjoins upon us, He Himself first of all does. – *Chapter 8*

Irenaeus

Against Heresies Book I

WE are saved, indeed, by means of faith and love; but all other things, while in their nature indifferent, are reckoned by the opinion of men—some good and some evil, there being nothing really evil by nature. – *Chapter 25*

Against Heresies Book II

IT is therefore better and more profitable to belong to the simple and unlettered class, and by means of love to attain to nearness to God, than, by imagining ourselves learned and skillful, to be found among those who are blasphemous against their own God, inasmuch as they conjure up another God as the Father. – *Chapter 26*

Against Heresies Book III

FOR the love of God, being rich and ungrudging, confers upon the suppliant more than he can ask from it. – *Preface*

WHEREFORE they know Him to whom the Son reveals Him; and again, the Father, by means of the Son, gives knowledge of His Son to those who love Him. – *Chapter 11*

FOR our love, inasmuch as it is true, is salutary to them, if they will but receive it. It may be compared to a severe remedy, extirpating the proud and sloughing flesh of a wound; for it puts an end to their pride and haughtiness. – *Chapter 25*

Against Heresies Book IV

FOR as we do direct our faith towards the Son, so also should we possess a firm and immovable love towards the Father. – *Chapter 6*

AND as their love towards God increases, He bestows more and greater gifts. – *Chapter 9*

HE did not Himself bring down from heaven any other commandment greater than this one, but renewed this very same one to His disciples, when He enjoined them to love God with all their heart, and others as themselves. – *Chapter 12*

THAT apart from the love of God, neither knowledge avails anything, nor the understanding of mysteries, nor faith, nor prophecy, but that without love all are hollow and vain; moreover, that love makes man perfect; and that he who loves God is perfect, both in this world and in that which is to come. For we do never cease from loving God; but in proportion as we continue to contemplate Him, so much the more do we love Him. – *Chapter 12*

AS in the law, therefore, and in the Gospel likewise, the first and greatest commandment is, to love the Lord God with the whole heart, and then there follows a commandment like to it, to love one's neighbor as one's self; the author of the law and the Gospel is shown to be one and the same. – *Chapter 12*

HE prohibited anger; and instead of the law enjoining the giving of tithes, He told us to share all our possessions with the poor; and not to love our neighbors only, but even our enemies; and not merely to be liberal givers and bestowers, but even that we should present a gratuitous gift to those who take away our goods. – *Chapter 13*

FOR to yield assent to God, and to follow His Word, and to love Him above all, and one's neighbor as one's self (now man is neighbor to man), and to abstain from every evil deed, and all other things of a like nature which are common to both covenants, do reveal one and the same God. – *Chapter 13*

FOR it behooves us to make an oblation to God, and in all things to be found grateful to God our Maker, in a pure mind, and in faith without hypocrisy, in well-grounded hope, in fervent love, offering the first-fruits of His own created things. – *Chapter 18*

HE shall also judge those who give rise to schisms, who are destitute of the love of God, and who look to their own special advantage rather than to the unity of the Church. – *Chapter 33*

Against Heresies Book V

NOW, where there exists an increase of love, there a greater glory is wrought out by the power of God for those who love Him. – *Chapter 3*

AND to as many as continue in their love towards God, does He grant communion with Him. – *Chapter 27*

Hermas

Pastor Book II

FIRST of all there is faith, then fear of the Lord, love, concord, words of righteousness, truth, patience. Than these, nothing is better in the life of men. If any one attend to these, and restrain himself not from them, blessed is he in his life. – *Commandment 8*

Clement of Alexandria

Exhortation to the Heathen

YOU have, then, God's promise; you have His love: become partaker of His grace. – *Chapter 1*

BUT the Lord, in His love to man, invites all men to the knowledge of the truth, and for this end sends the Paraclete. – *Chapter 9*

THIS is the inheritance with which the eternal covenant of God invests us, conveying the everlasting gift of grace; and thus our loving Father—the true Father—ceases not to exhort, admonish, train, love us. – *Chapter 10*

HIS love bestows blessings on repentance. – *Chapter 10*

LET us haste, let us run, let us take His yoke, let us receive, to conduct us to immortality, the good charioteer of men. Let us love Christ. – *Chapter 12*

CVS pharmacy

extrabucks

$8.00

rewards

$8 off $40 your next purchase!

Expires 01/12/2020 (Up to $8.00 value)

7119 3877 2000 8006

Limit of one purchased-based coupon, i.e., $4 off $20 purchase. ExtraCare card required. See www.cvs.com/couponpolicy or policy at register for details.

ExtraCare Card #: *9118 00183019387720

CPN#: 168976

CVS pharmacy

extrabucks

$8.00

rewards

$8 off $40 your next purchase!

Expires 01/12/2020 (up to $8.00 value)

7119 3877 2000 8006

Limit of one purchased-based coupon, i.e., $4 off $20 purchase. ExtraCare card required. See www.cvs.com/couponpolicy or policy at register for details.

ExtraCare Card #: *9118 0018301933877720

CPN#: 168976

ENOUGH, methinks, of words, though, impelled by love to man, I might have gone on to pour out what I had from God, that I might exhort to what is the greatest of blessings—salvation. – *Chapter 12*

Instructor Book I

THUS to Christ the fulfilling of His Father's will was food; and to us infants, who drink the milk of the word of the heavens, Christ Himself is food. Hence seeking is called sucking; for to those babes that seek the Word, the Father's breasts of love supply milk. – *Chapter 6*

FOR the Word blended with love at once cures our passions and cleanses our sins. – *Chapter 6*

THE Lord the Instructor is most good and unimpeachable, sympathizing as He does from the exceeding greatness of His love with the nature of each man. – *Chapter 8*

IF then He hates none of the things which He has made, it follows that He loves them. Much more than the rest, and with reason, will He love man, the noblest of all objects created by Him, and a God-loving being. Therefore God is loving; consequently the Word is loving. – *Chapter 8*

BUT he who loves anything wishes to do it good. – *Chapter 8*

FOR those who speak with a man merely to please him, have little love for him, seeing they do not pain him; while those that speak for his good, though they inflict pain for the time, do him good for ever after. – *Chapter 9*

FOR He shows both things: both His divinity in His foreknowledge of what would take place, and His love in affording an opportunity for repentance to the self-determination of the soul. – *Chapter 9*

FOR if you do not receive His love, ye shall know His power. – *Chapter 9*

AND the nature of all that love was the source of righteousness—the cause, too, of His lighting up His sun, and sending down His own Son. – *Chapter 9*

BY Moses, too, by reason of the love He has to man, He promises a gift to those who hasten to salvation. – *Chapter 10*

OUR superintendence in instruction and discipline is the office of the Word, from whom we learn frugality and humility, and all that pertains to love of truth, love of man, and love of excellence. – *Chapter 12*

Instructor Book II

BUT love (agape) is in truth celestial food, the banquet of reason. – *Chapter 1*

HE who eats of this meal, the best of all, shall possess the kingdom of God, fixing his regards here on the holy assembly of love, the heavenly Church. Love, then, is something pure and worthy of God, and its work is communication. – *Chapter 1*

HERBS are not love, but our meals are to be taken with love. – *Chapter 1*

THE Lord lays the acceptable offering of love, the spiritual fragrance, on the altar. – *Chapter 8*

BUT more worthy of love is that: "I have: why should I not give to those who need?" – *Chapter 13*

Instructor Book III

THERE is, too, another beauty of men—love. – *Chapter 1*

LOVE of wealth displaces a man from the right mode of life, and induces him to cease from feeling shame at what is shameful. – *Chapter 7*

AND faith is the possession not of the wise according to the world, but of those according to God; and it is taught without letters; and its handbook, at once rude and divine, is called love—a spiritual book. – *Chapter 11*

WOMAN and man are to go to church decently attired, with natural step, embracing silence, possessing unfeigned love, pure in body, pure in heart, fit to pray to God. – *Chapter 11*

BUT love is not proved by a kiss, but by kindly feeling. – *Chapter 11*

Stromata Book I

THE love of good is characteristic of a soul which uses its high spirit for noble ends. – *Chapter 24*

Stromata Book II

FOR love, on account of its friendly alliance with faith, makes men believers; and faith, which is the foundation of love, in its turn introduces the doing of good. – *Chapter 6*

AND, in truth, faith is discovered, by us, to be the first movement towards salvation; after which fear, and hope, and repentance, advancing in company with temperance and patience, lead us to love and knowledge. – *Chapter 6*

NOW love turns out to be consent in what pertains to reason, life, and manners, or in brief, fellowship in life, or it is the intensity of friendship and of affection, with right reason, in the enjoyment of associates. – *Chapter 9*

AND akin to love is hospitality, being a congenial art devoted to the treatment of strangers. – *Chapter 9*

AND if the real man within us is the spiritual, philanthropy is brotherly love to those who participate, in the same spirit. – *Chapter 9*

AS, then, the days are a portion of life in its progress, so also fear is the beginning of love, becoming by development faith, then love. – *Chapter 12*

BLESSED then is he who is found possessed of faith, being, as he is, composed of love and fear. – *Chapter 12*

FOR the fear of God trains and restores to love; but the fear of the works of the devil has hatred dwelling along with it. – *Chapter 12*

FOR he shows love to one like himself, because of his love to the Creator of the human race. – *Chapter 18*

WE are taught that there are three kinds of friendship: and that of these the first and the best is that which results from virtue, for the love that is founded on reason is firm; that the second and intermediate is by way of recompense, and is social, liberal, and useful for life; for the friendship which is the result of favor is mutual. – *Chapter 19*

Stromata Book IV

WE call martyrdom perfection, not because the man comes to the end of his life as others, but because he has exhibited the perfect work of love. – *Chapter 4*

YOU see that martyrdom for love's sake is taught. – *Chapter 7*

THE first step to salvation is the instruction accompanied with fear, in consequence of which we abstain from what is wrong; and the second is hope, by reason of which we desire the best things; but love, as is fitting, perfects, by training now according to knowledge. – *Chapter 7*

THE perfect man ought therefore to practice love, and thence to haste to the divine friendship, fulfilling the commandments from love. – *Chapter 13*

THIS is love, to love God and our neighbor. – *Chapter 18*

Stromata Book V

THE righteous man will seek the discovery that flows from love, to which if he haste he prospers. – *Chapter 3*

AND the end of good and of life is to become a lover of God. – *Chapter 14*

Stromata Book VI

FOR He who suffered out of His love for us, would have suppressed no element of knowledge requisite for our instruction. – *Chapter 8*

FOR it is impossible that he who has been once made perfect by love, and feasts eternally and insatiably on the boundless joy of contemplation, should delight in small and groveling things. – *Chapter 9*

FOR by going away to the Lord, for the love he bears Him, though his tabernacle be visible on earth, he does not withdraw himself from life. – *Chapter 9*

AND he, who knows the sure comprehension of the future which there is in the circumstances, in which he is placed, by love goes to meet the future. – *Chapter 9*

AND love is the keeping of the commandments which lead to knowledge. And the keeping of them is the establishment of the commandments, from which immortality results. – *Chapter 15*

BUT from the fact that truth appertains not to all, it is veiled in manifold ways, causing the light to arise only on those who are initiated into knowledge, who seek the truth through love. – *Chapter 15*

Stromata Book VII

NOW that which is lovable leads, to the contemplation of itself, each one who, from love of knowledge, applies himself entirely to contemplation. – *Chapter 2*

BUT knowing the sovereign will, and possessing as soon as he prays, being brought into close contact with the almighty power, and earnestly desiring to be spiritual, through boundless love, he is united to the Spirit. – *Chapter 7*

Chapter Two

JOY

ϑoψ

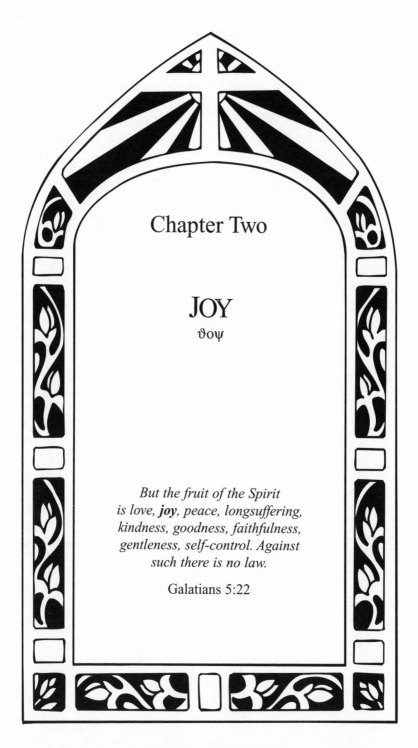

But the fruit of the Spirit
*is love, **joy**, peace, longsuffering,*
kindness, goodness, faithfulness,
gentleness, self-control. Against
such there is no law.

Galatians 5:22

Mathetes

Epistle to Diognetus

FOR it is not by ruling over his neighbors, or by seeking to hold the supremacy over those that are weaker, or by being rich, and showing violence towards those that are inferior, that happiness is found; nor can any one by these things become an imitator of God. – *Chapter 10*

Ignatius

Epistle to the Ephesians

FOR let us either fear the wrath to come, or let us love the present joy in the life that now is; and let our present and true joy be only this, to be found in Christ Jesus, that we may truly live. – *Chapter 11*

Epistle to the Magnesians

NEITHER endeavor that anything appear reasonable and proper to yourselves apart; but being come together into the same place, let there be one prayer, one supplication, one mind, one hope, in love and in joy undefiled. There is one Jesus Christ, than whom nothing is more excellent. – *Chapter 7*

Epistle to the Smyrnaeans

FOR the chief points are faith towards God, hope towards Christ, the enjoyment of those good things for which we look, and love towards God and our neighbor. – *Chapter 6*

Epistle to Polycarp

HAVING obtained good proof that thy mind is fixed in God as upon an immovable rock, I loudly glorify His name that I have been thought worthy to behold thy blameless face, which may I ever enjoy in God! – *Chapter 1*

Justin Martyr

First Apology

BUT our Jesus Christ, being crucified and dead, rose again, and having ascended to heaven, reigned; and by those things which were published in His name among all nations by the apostles, there is joy afforded to those who expect the immortality promised by Him. – *Chapter 42*

Irenaeus

Against Heresies Book II

THE body, therefore, does not cause the soul to forget those things which have been spiritually witnessed; but the soul teaches the body, and shares with it the spiritual vision which it has enjoyed. – *Chapter 33*

Against Heresies Book IV

AND for this purpose did the Father reveal the Son, that through His instrumentality He might be manifested to all, and might receive those righteous ones who believe in Him into incorruption and everlasting enjoyment (now, to believe in Him is to do His will). – *Chapter 6*

IT is not possible to live apart from life, and the means of life is found in fellowship with God; but fellowship with God is to know God, and to enjoy His goodness. – *Chapter 20*

Against Heresies Book V

FOR our face shall see the face of the Lord and shall rejoice with joy unspeakable—that is to say, when it shall behold its own delight. – *Chapter 7*

BUT communion with God is life and light, and the enjoyment of all the benefits which He has in store. – *Chapter 27*

Fragments

FOR then there shall in truth be a common joy consummated to all those who believe unto life, and in each individual shall be confirmed the mystery of the Resurrection, and the hope of incorruption, and the commencement of the eternal kingdom, when God shall have destroyed death and the devil. – *Chapter 50*

Hermas

Pastor Book III

They never, however, departed from God, but gladly bore His name, and joyfully received His servants into their houses. – *Similitude 8, Chapter 10*

For both he who is in want, and he who suffers inconveniences in his daily life, is in great torture and necessity. Whoever, therefore, rescues a soul of this kind from necessity, will gain for himself great joy. – *Similitude 10, Chapter 4*

Theophilus of Antioch

To Autolycus Book I

To those who by patient continuance in well-doing seek immortality, He will give life everlasting, joy, peace, rest, and abundance of good things, which neither hath eye seen, nor ear heard, nor hath it entered into the heart of man to conceive. – *Chapter 13*

Clement of Alexandria

Exhortation to the Heathen

He gives thee all creatures that fly and swim, and those on the land. These the Father has created for thy thankful enjoyment. – *Chapter 10*

Instructor Book I

Here is to be noted the mystery of the bread, inasmuch as He speaks of it as flesh, and as flesh, consequently, that has risen through fire, as the wheat springs up from decay and germination; and, in truth, it has risen through fire for the joy of the Church, as bread baked. – *Chapter 6*

Thus in many ways the Word is figuratively described, as meat, and flesh, and food, and bread, and blood, and milk. The Lord is all these, to give enjoyment to us who have believed on Him. – *Chapter 6*

It is not immediate pleasure, but future enjoyment, that the Lord has in view. – *Chapter 9*

Instructor Book II

And these joys have an inspiration of love from the public nutriment, which accustoms to everlasting dainties. – *Chapter 1*

And happiness is found in the practice of virtue. – *Chapter 1*

Finally, before partaking of sleep, it is a sacred duty to give thanks to God, having enjoyed His grace and love, and so go straight to sleep. – *Chapter 4*

As beauty, so also the flower delights when looked at; and it is meet to glorify the Creator by the enjoyment of the sight of beautiful objects. – *Chapter 8*

It becomes us who truly follow the Scripture to enjoy ourselves temperately, as in Paradise. – *Chapter 8*

For in reality simplicity provides for sanctity, by reducing redundancies to equality, and by furnishing from whatever is at hand the enjoyment sought from superfluities. – *Chapter 13*

Instructor Book III

But that is the better enjoyment which the Lord assigned to the disciple, when He taught him to "catch men" as fishes in the water. – *Chapter 10*

Stromata Book II

For He does not allow us either to grieve at our neighbor's good, or to reap joy at our neighbor's ill. – *Chapter 18*

Stromata Book IV

To the whole human race, then, discipline and virtue are a necessity, if they would pursue after happiness. – *Chapter 8*

And the happiness of marriage ought never to be estimated either by wealth or beauty, but by virtue. – *Chapter 20*

But he who obeys the mere call, as he is called, neither for fear, nor for enjoyments, is on his way to knowledge. – *Chapter 22*

Stromata Book V

And if we live throughout holily and righteously, we are happy here, and shall be happier after our departure hence; not possessing happiness for a time, but enabled to rest in eternity. – *Chapter 14*

Stromata Book VI

For the use and enjoyment of necessaries are not injurious in quality, but in quantity, when in excess. – Chapter 12

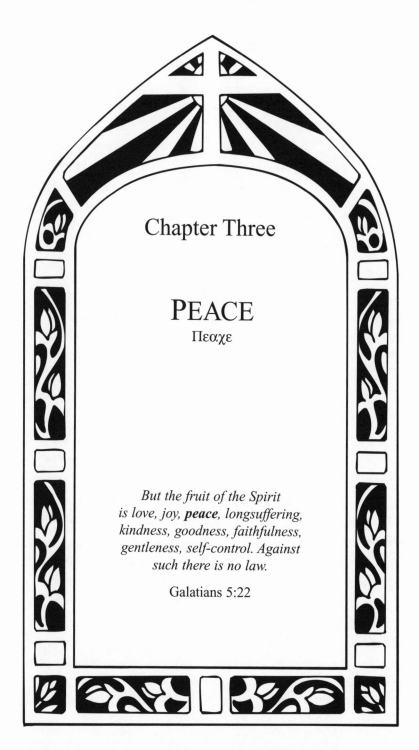

Chapter Three

PEACE

Πεαχε

But the fruit of the Spirit
*is love, joy, **peace**, longsuffering,*
kindness, goodness, faithfulness,
gentleness, self-control. Against
such there is no law.

Galatians 5:22

Clement of Rome

First Epistle to the Corinthians

Thus a profound and abundant peace was given to you all, and ye had an insatiable desire for doing good, while a full outpouring of the Holy Spirit was upon you all. – *Chapter 2*

If thou offerest rightly, but dost not divide rightly, hast thou not sinned? Be at peace: thine offering returns to thyself, and thou shalt again possess it. – *Chapter 4*

Let us cleave, therefore, to those who cultivate peace with godliness, and not to those who hypocritically profess to desire it. – *Chapter 15*

The chastisement of our peace was upon Him, and by His stripes we were healed. – *Chapter 16*

Wherefore, having so many great and glorious examples set before us, let us turn again to the practice of that peace which from the beginning was the mark set before us; and let us look steadfastly to the Father and Creator of the universe, and cleave to His mighty and surpassingly great gifts and benefactions of peace. – *Chapter 19*

The heavens, revolving under His government, are subject to Him in peace. – *Chapter 20*

The very smallest of living beings meet together in peace and concord. All these the great Creator and Lord of all has appointed to exist in peace and harmony. – *Chapter 20*

Depart from evil, and do good; seek peace, and pursue it. The eyes of the Lord are upon the righteous, and His ears are open unto their prayers. – *Chapter 22*

Only let the flock of Christ live on terms of peace with the presbyters set over it. – *Chapter 54*

Ignatius

Epistle to the Ephesians

Nothing is more precious than peace, by which all war, both in heaven and earth, is brought to an end. – *Chapter 13*

Epistle to the Smyrnaeans

What appears to me proper to be done is this, that you should send some one of your number with an epistle, so that, in company with them, he may rejoice over the tranquillity which, according to the will of God, they have obtained, and because that, through your prayers, I have secured Christ as a safe harbor. – *Chapter 11*

Grace, mercy, peace, and patience, be with you in Christ forevermore! – *Chapter 12*

Second Epistle to the Ephesians

Against their fierceness be ye peaceful and quiet, and be ye not astounded by them. Let us, then, be imitators of our Lord in meekness, and strive who shall more especially be injured, and oppressed, and defrauded. – *Chapter 10*

Epistle to the Antiochians

The Lord has rendered my bonds light and easy since I learnt that you are in peace, and that you live in all harmony both of the flesh and spirit. – *Chapter 1*

Barnabas

Epistle

Thou shalt be meek: thou shalt be peaceable. – *Chapter 19*

Justin Martyr

First Apology

And more than all other men are we your helpers and allies in promoting peace, seeing that we hold this view, that it is alike impossible for the wicked, the covetous, the conspirator, and for the virtuous, to escape the notice of God, and that each man goes to everlasting punishment or salvation according to the value of his actions. – *Chapter 12*

Discourse to the Greeks

Lust being once banished, the soul becomes calm and serene. – *Chapter 5*

Irenaeus

Against Heresies Book III

For, after our Lord rose from the dead, the apostles were invested with power from on high when the Holy Spirit came down upon them, were filled from all His gifts, and had perfect knowledge: they departed to the ends of the earth, preaching the glad tidings of the good things sent from God to us, and proclaiming the peace of heaven to men, who indeed do all equally and individually possess the Gospel of God. – *Chapter 1*

Against Heresies Book IV

For, after the wind which rends the mountains, and after the earthquake, and after the fire, come the tranquil and peaceful times of His kingdom, in which the spirit of God does, in the most gentle manner, vivify and increase mankind. – *Chapter 20*

Men who prate of peace while they give rise to war, and do in truth strain out a gnat, but swallow a camel. – *Chapter 33*

Keep thy tongue from evil, and thy lips that they speak no guile; depart from evil, and do good; seek peace, and pursue it. – *Chapter 36*

Fragments

And this variety among the observers of the fasts had not its origin in our time, but long before in that of our predecessors, some of whom probably, being not very accurate in their observance of it, handed down to posterity the custom as it had, through simplicity or private fancy, been introduced among them. And yet nevertheless all these lived in peace one with another, and we also keep peace together. Thus, in fact, the difference in observing the fast establishes the harmony of our common faith. – *Chapter 3*

Hermas

Pastor Book I

Now, therefore, listen to me, and be at peace one with another, and visit each other, and bear each other's burdens, and do not partake of God's creatures alone, but give abundantly of them to the needy. – *Chapter 9*

Instruct each other therefore, and be at peace among yourselves, that I also, standing joyful before your Father, may give an account of you all to your Lord. – *Chapter 9*

Pastor Book II

For slander is evil and an unsteady demon. It never abides in peace, but always remains in discord. Keep yourself from it, and you will always be at peace with all. – *Commandment 2*

But patience is great, and mighty, and strong, and calm in the midst of great enlargement, joyful, rejoicing, free from care, glorifying God at all times, having no bitterness in her, and abiding continually meek and quiet. – *Commandment 5, Chapter 2*

The tender Spirit, then, not being accustomed to dwell with the wicked spirit, nor with hardness, withdraws from such a man, and seeks to dwell with meekness and peacefulness. – *Commandment 5, Chapter 2*

First, he who has the Divine Spirit proceeding from above is meek, and peaceable, and humble, and refrains from all iniquity and the vain desire of this world, and contents himself with fewer wants than those of other men, and when asked he makes no reply; nor does he speak privately, nor when man wishes the spirit to speak does the Holy Spirit speak, but it speaks only when God wishes it to speak. – *Commandment 11*

Pastor Book III

Heal yourselves, therefore, while the tower is still building. The Lord dwells in men that love peace, because He loved peace; but from the contentious and the utterly wicked He is far distant. – *Similitude 9, Chapter 32*

Theophilus of Antioch

To Autolycus Book I

To those who by patient continuance in well-doing seek immortality, He will give life everlasting, joy, peace, rest, and abundance of good things, which neither hath eye seen, nor ear heard, nor hath it entered into the heart of man to conceive. – *Chapter 14*

Athenagoras

A Plea for the Christians

And this is also for our advantage, that we may lead a peaceable and quiet life, and may ourselves readily perform all that is commanded us. – *Chapter 33*

Clement of Alexandria

Exhortation to the Heathen

Whence He was and what He was, He showed by what He taught and exhibited, manifesting Himself as the Herald of the Covenant, the Reconciler, our Savior, the Word, the Fount of life, the Giver of peace, diffused over the whole face of the earth; by whom, so to speak, the universe has already become an ocean of blessings. – *Chapter 10*

And shall not Christ, breathing a strain of peace to the ends of the earth, gather together His own soldiers, the soldiers of peace? Well, by His blood, and by the word, He has gathered the bloodless host of peace, and assigned to them the kingdom of heaven. – *Chapter 11*

Instructor Book I

Thus also He who is our great General, the Word, the Commander-in-chief of the universe by admonishing those who throw off the restraints of His law, that He may effect their release from the slavery, error, and captivity of the adversary, brings them peacefully to the sacred concord of citizenship. – *Chapter 8*

For where the face of the Lord looks, there is peace and rejoicing; but where it is averted, there is the introduction of evil. The Lord, accordingly, does not wish to look on evil things; for He is good. – *Chapter 8*

For it is not in war, but in peace, that we are trained. War needs great preparation, and luxury craves profusion; but peace and love, simple and quiet sisters, require no arms nor excessive preparation. The Word is their sustenance. – *Chapter 12*

Instructor Book II

But we, the people of peace, feasting for lawful enjoyment, not to wantonness, drink sober cups of friendship, that our friendships may be shown in a way truly appropriate to the name. – *Chapter 2*

The one instrument of peace, the Word alone by which we honor God, is what we employ. – *Chapter 4*

In a word, the Christian is characterized by composure, tranquillity, calmness, and peace. – *Chapter 7*

The crown is the symbol of untroubled tranquillity. – *Chapter 8*

Instructor Book III

And it becomes him who is rightly trained, on whom peace has pitched its tent, to preserve peace also with his hair. – *Chapter 3*

To men of peace and of light, therefore, white is appropriate. – *Chapter 11*

Stromata Book I

Those who peacefully contemplate sacred things are in manifold ways trained to their calling. – *Chapter 5*

For the shepherd's life is a preparation for sovereignty in the case of him who is destined to rule over the peaceful flock of men, as the chase for those who are by nature warlike. – *Chapter 23*

Stromata Book II

But peace with one another and kindly feeling are what is best. *Chapter 5*

Faith, and knowledge, and peace are delight, from which he that has disobeyed is cast out. – *Chapter 11*

And enemies, although drawn up before the walls attempting to take the city, are not to be regarded as enemies till they are by the voice of the herald summoned to peace. – *Chapter 18*

For peace and freedom are not otherwise won, than by ceaseless and unyielding struggles with our lusts. – *Chapter 20*

Stromata Book IV

It follows that the perfect peacemaking is that which keeps unchanged in all circumstances what is peaceful; calls Providence holy and good; and has its being in the knowledge of divine and human affairs, by which it deems the opposites that are in the world to be the fairest harmony of creation. They also are peacemakers, who teach those who war against the stratagems of sin to have recourse to faith and peace. – *Chapter 6*

So, then, what is really good is seen to be most pleasant, and of itself produces the fruit which is desired—tranquillity of soul. – *Chapter 23*

Righteousness is peace of life and a well-conditioned state. – *Chapter 25*

And Melchizedek is interpreted "righteous king"; and the name is a synonym for righteousness and peace. – *Chapter 25*

Stromata Book VI

Epicurus says, "The greatest fruit of righteousness is tranquillity." – *Chapter 2*

Wherefore He moves those who are adapted to useful exertion in the things which pertain to virtue, and peace, and beneficence. But all that is characterized by virtue proceeds from virtue, and leads back to virtue. – *Chapter 17*

Stromata Book VII

Maintaining prudence, he exercises moderation in the calmness of his soul. – *Chapter 3*

Fragments

In the prayer which is made at home, after rising from prayer, the salutation of joy is also the token of peace. – *Chapter 4*

Nicetas Bishop of Heraclea

From His Catena

Calmness is a thing which, of all other things, is most to be prized. – *Chapter 2*

Chapter Four

LONGSUFFERING

Πεαχε

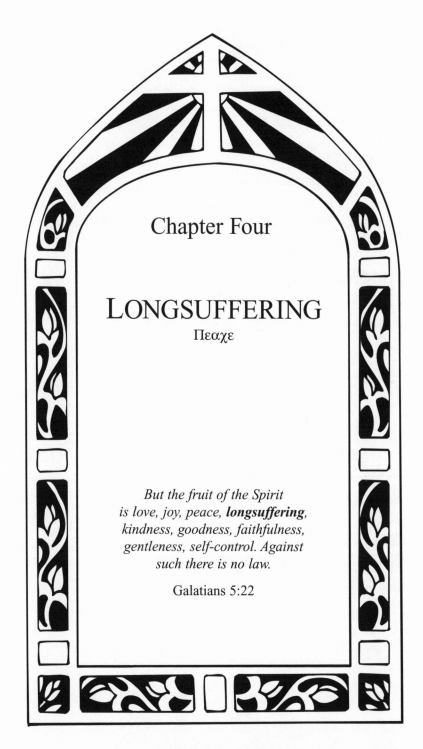

But the fruit of the Spirit
is love, joy, peace, ***longsuffering****,*
kindness, goodness, faithfulness,
gentleness, self-control. Against
such there is no law.

Galatians 5:22

Clement of Rome

First Epistle to the Corinthians

Let us contemplate Him with our understanding, and look with the eyes of our soul to His longsuffering will. Let us reflect how free from wrath He is towards all His creation. – *Chapter 19*

Polycarp

Epistle to the Philippians

Let us then be imitators of His patience; and if we suffer for His name's sake, let us glorify Him. For He has set us this example in Himself, and we have believed that such is the case. – *Chapter 8*

Ignatius

Epistle to the Ephesians

If any one, the more he is injured, displays the more patience, blessed is he. – *Chapter 10*

The last times are come upon us. Let us therefore be of a reverent spirit, and fear the longsuffering of God, that it tend not to our condemnation. – *Chapter 11*

Third Epistle

Be ye perfectly strong in the patience of Jesus Christ our God. – *Chapter 9*

Epistle to Polycarp

Bear with all men, even as our Lord beareth with thee. Show patience with all men in love, as indeed thou doest. – *Chapter 1*

Epistle to the Deacon Hero of Antioch

Be longsuffering, that thou mayest be great in wisdom. – *Chapter 5*

Barnabas

Epistle

Fear and patience, then, are helpers of our faith; and longsuffering and continence are things which fight on our side. While these remain pure in what respects the Lord, Wisdom, Understanding, Science, and Knowledge rejoice along with them. – *Chapter 2*

To this end, therefore, brethren, He is longsuffering, foreseeing how the people whom He has prepared shall with guilelessness believe in His Beloved. – *Chapter 3*

Justin Martyr

First Apology

For we ought not to strive; neither has He desired us to be imitators of wicked men, but He has exhorted us to lead all men, by patience and gentleness, from shame and the love of evil. – *Chapter 16*

Dialogue with Trypho, A Jew

But we pray that even now all of you may repent and obtain mercy from God, the compassionate and longsuffering Father of all. – *Chapter 108*

Irenaeus

Against Heresies Book III

But as our Lord is alone truly Master, so the Son of God is truly good and patient, the Word of God the Father having been made the Son of man. – *Chapter 18*

Longsuffering therefore was God, when man became a defaulter, as foreseeing that victory which should be granted to him through the Word. – *Chapter 20*

Hermas

Pastor Book II

For if you be patient, the Holy Spirit that dwells in you will be pure. – *Commandment 5, Chapter 1*

You see, then, that patience is sweeter than honey, and useful to God, and the Lord dwells in it. But anger is bitter and useless. – *Commandment 5, Chapter 1*

But patience is great, and mighty, and strong, and calm in the midst of great enlargement, joyful, rejoicing, free from care, glorifying God at all times, having no bitterness in her, and abiding continually meek and quiet. – *Commandment 5, Chapter 2*

Wherefore do you depart from that most wicked spirit anger, and put on patience, and resist anger and bitterness, and you will be found in company with the purity which is loved by the Lord. – *Commandment 5, Chapter 2*

Pastor Book III

Life is the possession of all who keep the commandments of the Lord; but in the commandments there is no rivalry in regard to the first places, or glory of any kind, but in regard to patience and personal humility. – S*imilitude 8, Chapter 7*

Clement of Alexandria

Stromata Book II

And, in truth, faith is discovered, by us, to be the first movement towards salvation; after which fear, and hope, and repentance, advancing in company with temperance and patience, lead us to love and knowledge. – *Chapter 6*

Fear and patience are then helpers of your faith; and our allies are longsuffering and temperance. – *Chapter 6*

The merciful man is longsuffering; and in every one who shows solicitude there is wisdom. – *Chapter 18*

Stromata Book IV

For ye have need of patience, that, after doing the will of God, ye may obtain the promise. For yet a little while, and He that cometh will come, and will not tarry. – *Chapter 16*

Stromata Book VII

Whence he is always mild and meek, accessible, affable, longsuffering, grateful, endued with a good conscience. Such a man is rigid, not alone so as not to be corrupted, but so as not to be tempted. – *Chapter 7*

Nicetas Bishop of Heraclea

From His Catena

For truly enviable, and, in my judgment, worthy of all admiration, a man is, if he has attained to such a degree of longsuffering as to be able with ease to grapple with the pain, truly keen, and not easily conquered by everybody, which arises from being wronged. – *Chapter 2*

Chapter Five

KINDNESS

Κινδνεσσ

But the fruit of the Spirit
is love, joy, peace, longsuffering,
***kindness**, goodness, faithfulness,*
gentleness, self-control. Against
such there is no law.

Galatians 5:22

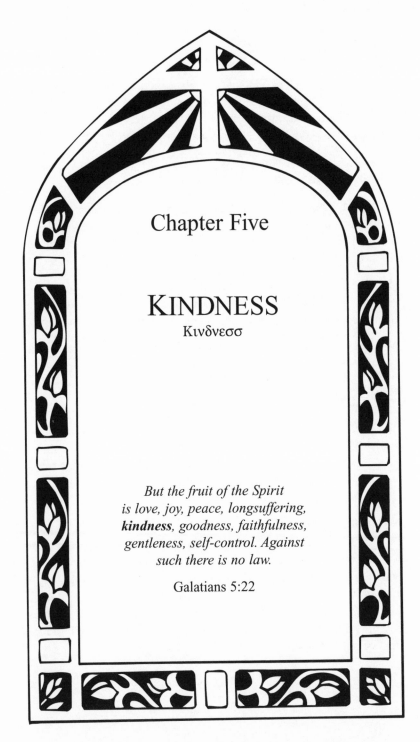

Clement of Rome

First Epistle to the Corinthians

Wherefore, let us yield obedience to His excellent and glorious will; and imploring His mercy and loving-kindness, while we forsake all fruitless labors, and strife, and envy, which leads to death, let us turn and have recourse to His compassions. – *Chapter 9*

Let us be kind one to another after the pattern of the tender mercy and benignity of our Creator. – *Chapter 14*

Take heed, beloved, lest His many kindnesses lead to the condemnation of us all. For thus it must be unless we walk worthy of Him, and with one mind do those things which are good and well-pleasing in His sight. – *Chapter 21*

The all-merciful and beneficent Father has bowels of compassion towards those that fear Him, and kindly and lovingly bestows His favors upon those who come to Him with a simple mind. – *Chapter 23*

Who then among you is noble-minded? who compassionate? who full of love? – *Chapter 54*

Polycarp

Epistle to the Philippians

They [the deacons] must not be slanderers, double-tongued, or lovers of money, but temperate in all things, compassionate, industrious, walking according to the truth of the Lord, who was the servant of all. – *Chapter 5*

And let the presbyters be compassionate and merciful to all, bringing back those that wander, visiting all the sick, and not neglecting the widow, the orphan, or the poor, but always "providing for that which is becoming in the sight of God and man"; abstaining from all wrath, respect of persons, and unjust judgment; keeping far off from all covetousness, not quickly crediting an evil report against any one, not severe in judgment, as knowing that we are all under a debt of sin. – *Chapter 6*

Ignatius

Epistle to the Ephesians

Let us make them brethren by our kindness. For say ye to those that hate you, Ye are our brethren, that the name of the Lord may be glorified. – *Chapter 10*

Epistle to the Magnesians

Let us not, therefore, be insensible to His kindness. For were He to reward us according to our works, we should cease to be. Therefore, having become His disciples, let us learn to live according to the principles of Christianity. – *Chapter 10*

Epistle to the Philadelphians

I therefore exhort you in the Lord to receive with all tenderness those that repent and return to the unity of the Church, that through your kindness and forbearance they may recover themselves out of the snare of the devil, and becoming worthy of Jesus Christ, may obtain eternal salvation in the kingdom of Christ. – *Chapter 3*

Epistle to the Smyrnaeans

God will recompense you, for whose sake ye have shown such kindness towards His prisoner. For even if I am not worthy of it, yet your zeal to help me is an admirable thing. – *Chapter 9*

Barnabas

Epistle

I beseech you who are superiors, if you will receive any counsel of my goodwill, have among yourselves those to whom you may show kindness: do not forsake them. – *Chapter 21*

Justin Martyr

Dialogue with Trypho, A Jew

He urged all who fear God to praise Him because He had compassion on all races of believing men, through the mystery of Him who was crucified. – *Chapter 106*

Irenaeus

Against Heresies Book II

For God is superior to nature, and has in Himself the disposition to show kindness, because He is good; and the ability to do so, because He is mighty; and the faculty of fully carrying out His purpose, because He is rich and perfect. – *Chapter 29*

But in the Church, sympathy, and compassion, and steadfastness, and truth, for the aid and encouragement of mankind, are not only displayed without fee or reward, but we ourselves lay out for the benefit of others our own means. – *Chapter 31*

Against Heresies Book III

And from this fact, that He exclaimed upon the cross, "Father, forgive them, for they know not what they do," the longsuffering, patience, compassion, and goodness of Christ are exhibited, since He both suffered, and did Himself exculpate those who had maltreated Him. – *Chapter 18*

For, when strength was made perfect in weakness, it showed the kindness and transcendent power of God. – *Chapter 20*

The sense of sin leads to repentance, and God bestows His compassion upon those who are penitent. – *Chapter 23*

Against Heresies Book IV

For it was not because He was angry, like a man, as many venture to say, that He rejected their sacrifices; but out of compassion to their blindness, and with the view of suggesting to them the true sacrifice, by offering which they shall appease God, that they may receive life from Him. – *Chapter 7*

For the Father is incomprehensible; but in regard to His love, and kindness, and as to His infinite power, even this He grants to those who love Him, that is, to see God, which thing the prophets did also predict. – *Chapter 20*

His wisdom is shown in His having made created things parts of one harmonious and consistent whole; and those things which, through His supereminent kindness, receive growth and a long period of existence, do reflect the glory of the uncreated One, of that God who bestows what is good ungrudgingly. – *Chapter 38*

Against Heresies Book V

Since He was man, and since He was God, in order that since as man He suffered for us, so as God He might have compassion on us, and forgive us our debts, in which we were made debtors to God our Creator. – *Chapter 17*

Fragments

He kindly welcomes and accepts them as premature fruits, and honors the mind, whatsoever it may be, which is stamped with virtue, although not yet perfect. – *Chapter 55*

Hermas

Pastor Book I

For the Lord had compassion on you, and renewed your spirit, and ye laid aside your infirmities. – *Vision 3, Chapter 12*

Pastor Book III

But those who are weak and slothful in prayer, hesitate to ask anything from the Lord; but the Lord is full of compassion, and gives without fail to all who ask Him. – *Similitude 5, Chapter 4*

Theophilus of Antioch

To Autolycus Book II

And, for the rest, would that in a kindly spirit you would investigate divine things—I mean the things that are spoken by the prophets—in order that, by comparing what is said by us with the utterances of the others, you may be able to discover the truth. – *Chapter 34*

Clement of Alexandria

Instructor Book I

Now censure is a mark of good will, not of ill will. For both he who is a friend and he who is not, reproach; but the enemy does so in scorn, the friend in kindness. It is not, then, from hatred that the Lord chides men; for He Himself suffered for us, whom He might have destroyed for our faults. – *Chapter 8*

Instructor Book III

But the compassionate God Himself set the flesh free, and releasing it from destruction, and from bitter and deadly bondage, endowed it with incorruptibility, arraying the flesh in this, the holy embellishment of eternity—immortality. – *Chapter 1*

So fairness, and forbearance, and kindness, are what well becomes the masters. – *Chapter 11*

But love is not proved by a kiss, but by kindly feeling. – *Chapter 11*

Stromata Book I

It is essential, certainly, that the providence which manages all, be both supreme and good. For it is the power of both that dispenses salvation—the one correcting by punishment, as supreme, the other showing kindness in the exercise of beneficence, as a benefactor. – *Chapter 27*

Stromata Book II

Besides, the tithes of the fruits and of the flocks taught both piety towards the Deity, and not covetously to grasp everything, but to communicate gifts of kindness to one's neighbors. – *Chapter 18*

Stromata Book IV

For ye had compassion of me in my bonds, and took with joy the spoiling of your goods, knowing that you have a better and enduring substance. Cast not away therefore your confidence, which hath great recompense of reward. – *Chapter 16*

Stromata Book V

For the Word of the Father of the universe is not the uttered word, but the wisdom and most manifest kindness of God, and His power too, which is almighty and truly divine, and not incapable of being conceived by those who do not confess—the all-potent will. – *Chapter 1*

Who Is the Rich Man That Shall Be Saved?

For truly such is God's delight in giving. And this saying is above all divinity—not to wait to be asked, but to inquire oneself who deserves to receive kindness. – *Chapter 31*

Open thy compassion to all who are enrolled the disciples of God; not looking contemptuously to personal appearance, nor carelessly disposed to any period of life. Nor if one appears penniless, or ragged, or ugly, or feeble, do thou fret in soul at this and turn away. – *Chapter 33*

All these warriors and guards are trusty. No one is idle, no one is useless. One can obtain your pardon from God, another comfort you when sick, another weep and groan in sympathy for you to the Lord of all, another teach some of the things useful for salvation, another admonish with confidence, another counsel with kindness. – *Chapter 35*

Chapter Six

GOODNESS

Γοοδνεσσ

But the fruit of the Spirit
is love, joy, peace, longsuffering,
kindness, ***goodness****, faithfulness,*
gentleness, self-control. Against
such there is no law.

Galatians 5:22

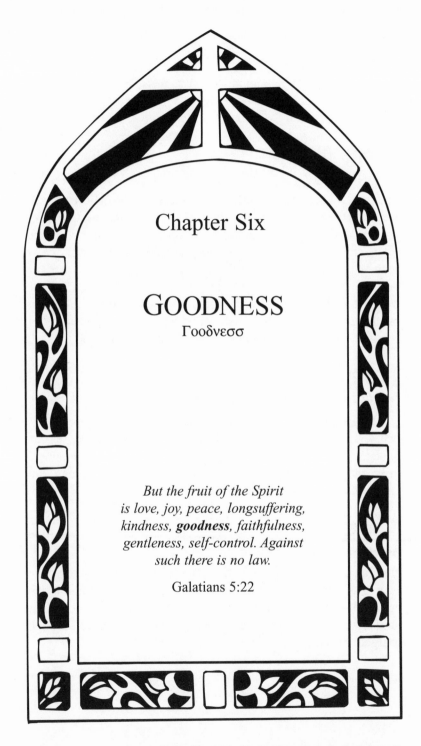

Ignatius

Epistle to the Ephesians

The last times are come upon us. Let us therefore be of a reverent spirit, and fear the longsuffering of God, lest we despise the riches of His goodness and forbearance. – *Chapter 11*

Justin Martyr

First Apology

And we have been taught, and are convinced, and do believe, that He accepts those only who imitate the excellences which reside in Him, temperance, and justice, and philanthropy, and as many virtues as are peculiar to a God who is called by no proper name. And we have been taught that He in the beginning did of His goodness, for man's sake, create all things out of unformed matter; and if men by their works show themselves worthy of this His design, they are deemed worthy, and so we have received—of reigning in company with Him, being delivered from corruption and suffering. – *Chapter 10*

Justin Martyr

Dialogue with Trypho, A Jew

For the goodness and the loving-kindness of God, and His boundless riches, hold righteous and sinless the man who, as Ezekiel tells, repents of sins; and reckons sinful, unrighteous, and impious the man who falls away from piety and righteousness to unrighteousness and ungodliness. – *Chapter 47*

Irenaeus

Against Heresies Book I

Not that I am practiced either in composition or eloquence; but my feeling of affection prompts me to make known to thee and all thy companions those doctrines which have been kept in concealment until now, but which are at last, through the goodness of God, brought to light. – *Preface*

Against Heresies Book II

For with the name of God the following words will harmonize: intelligence, word, life, incorruption, truth, wisdom, goodness, and such like. – *Chapter 13*

For thou, O man, art not an uncreated being, nor didst thou always coexist with God, as did His own Word; but now, through His preeminent goodness, receiving the beginning of thy creation, thou dost gradually learn from the Word the dispensations of God who made thee. – *Chapter 25*

Against Heresies Book III

On the other hand, the good God, if he is merely good, and not one who tests those upon whom he shall send his goodness, will be out of the range of justice and goodness; and his goodness will seem imperfect, as not saving all; for it should do so, if it be not accompanied with judgment. – *Chapter 25*

For he that is the judicial one, if he be not good, is not God, because he from whom goodness is absent is no God at all; and again, he who is good, if he has no judicial power, suffers the same loss as the former, by being deprived of his character of deity. – *Chapter 25*

For He is good, and merciful, and patient, and saves whom He ought: nor does goodness desert Him in the exercise of justice, nor is His wisdom lessened; for He saves those whom He should save, and judges those worthy of judgment. Neither does He show Himself unmercifully just; for His goodness, no doubt, goes on before, and takes precedence. – *Chapter 25*

Against Heresies Book IV

For the receptacle of His goodness, and the instrument of His glorification, is the man who is grateful to Him that made him. – *Chapter 11*

But that no one can fully declare the goodness of God from the things made by Him, is a point evident to all. – *Chapter 19*

For as His greatness is past finding out, so also His goodness is beyond expression; by which having been seen, He bestows life upon those who see Him. It is not possible to live apart from life, and the means of life is found in fellowship with God; but fellowship with God is to know God, and to enjoy His goodness. – *Chapter 20*

God thus determining all things beforehand for the bringing of man to perfection, for his edification, and for the revelation of His dispensations, that goodness may both be made apparent, and righteousness perfected, and that the Church may be fashioned after the image of His Son, and that man may finally be brought to maturity at some future time, becoming ripe through such privileges to see and comprehend God. – *Chapter 37*

With God there are simultaneously exhibited power, wisdom, and goodness. His power and goodness appear in this, that of His own will He called into being and fashioned things having no previous existence. – *Chapter 38*

For creation is an attribute of the goodness of God; but to be created is that of human nature. – *Chapter 39*

Hermas

Pastor Book II

Practice goodness; and from the rewards of your labors, which God gives you, give to all the needy in simplicity, not hesitating as to whom you are to give or not to give. – *Commandment 2*

For empty jars quickly become sour, and the goodness of the wine is gone. So also the devil goes to all the servants of God to try them. – *Commandment 12, Chapter 5*

Theophilus of Antioch

To Autolycus Book I

For in glory He is incomprehensible, in greatness unfathomable, in height inconceivable, in power incomparable, in wisdom unrivaled, in goodness inimitable, in kindness unutterable. – *Chapter 3*

Clement of Alexandria

Exhortation to the Heathen

And you know not that, of all truths, this is the truest, that the good and godly shall obtain the good reward, inasmuch as they held goodness in high esteem; while, on the other hand, the wicked shall receive meet punishment. – *Chapter 10*

The heavenly and truly divine love comes to men thus, when in the soul itself the spark of true goodness, kindled in the soul by the Divine Word, is able to burst forth into flame. – *Chapter 11*

Instructor Book I

And we are tender who are pliant to the power of persuasion, and are easily drawn to goodness, and are mild, and free of the stain of malice and perverseness, for the ancient race was perverse and hard-hearted; but the band of infants, the new people which we are, is delicate as a child. – *Chapter 5*

That which does good must be every way better than that which does not good. But nothing is better than the Good. The Good, then, does good. And God is admitted to be good. God therefore does good. And the Good, in virtue of its being good, does nothing else than do good. Consequently God does all good. – *Chapter 8*

Righteousness, therefore, has characteristics corresponding to all the aspects in which goodness is examined, both possessing equal properties equally. And things which are characterized by equal properties are equal and similar to each other. Righteousness is therefore a good thing. – *Chapter 8*

God, then, is good. And the Lord speaks many a time and oft before He proceeds to act. – *Chapter 8*

See how God, through His love of goodness, seeks repentance; and by means of the plan He pursues of threatening silently, shows His own love for man. – *Chapter 8*

And it is the prerogative of goodness to save. – *Chapter 9*

Thus He knew that they turned for fear, while they despised His love: for, for the most part, that goodness which is always mild is despised; but He who admonishes by the loving fear of righteousness is reverenced. – *Chapter 9*

Do you see the goodness of justice, in that it counsels to repentance? – *Chapter 10*

Honey, being very sweet, generates bile, as goodness begets contempt, which is the cause of sinning. But mustard lessens bile, that is, anger, and stops inflammation, that is, pride. From which Word springs the true health of the soul, and its eternal happy temperament. – *Chapter 11*

Instructor Book II

It is highly requisite for the men who belong to us to give forth the odor not of ointments, but of nobleness and goodness. – *Chapter 8*

Instructor Book III

It is not, then, the aspect of the outward man, but the soul that is to be decorated with the ornament of goodness; we may say also the flesh with the adornment of temperance. – *Chapter 2*

Stromata Book II

But God being by nature rich in pity, in consequence of His own goodness, cares for us, though neither portions of Himself, nor by nature His children. And this is the greatest proof of the goodness of God: that such being our relation to Him, and being by nature wholly estranged, He nevertheless cares for us. – *Chapter 16*

You see how the law proclaims at once the righteousness and goodness of God, who dispenses food to all ungrudgingly. – *Chapter 18*

Stromata Book V

But the good differ especially from the bad in inclinations and good desires. – *Chapter 13*

Stromata Book VI

For what is the use of good that does not act and do good? – *Chapter 12*

For God's righteousness is good, and His goodness is righteous. – *Chapter 14*

Since many advantages are common to good and bad men: yet they are nevertheless advantageous only to men of goodness and probity, for whose sake God created them. For it was for the use of good men that the influence which is in God's gifts was originated. – *Chapter 17*

Stromata Book VII

But necessary corrections, through the goodness of the great overseeing Judge, both by the attendant angels, and by various acts of anticipative judgment, and by the perfect judgment, compel egregious sinners to repent. – *Chapter 2*

And others there are, who are persuaded that those they reckon gods are capable of being prevailed upon by sacrifices and gifts, favoring, so to speak, their profligacies; and will not believe that He is the only true God, who exists in the invariableness of righteous goodness. – *Chapter 3*

But if one say to us, that some sinners even obtain according to their requests, we should say that this rarely takes place, by reason of the righteous goodness of God. And it is granted to those who are capable of doing others good. – *Chapter 12*

Ye have cast off the passions of the soul, in order to become assimilated, as far as possible, to the goodness of God's providence by longsuffering, and by forgiveness "towards the just and the unjust," casting on them the gleam of benignity in word and deeds, as the sun. – *Chapter 14*

"Forgive, and it shall be forgiven you"; the commandment, as it were, compelling to salvation through superabundance of goodness. – *Chapter 14*

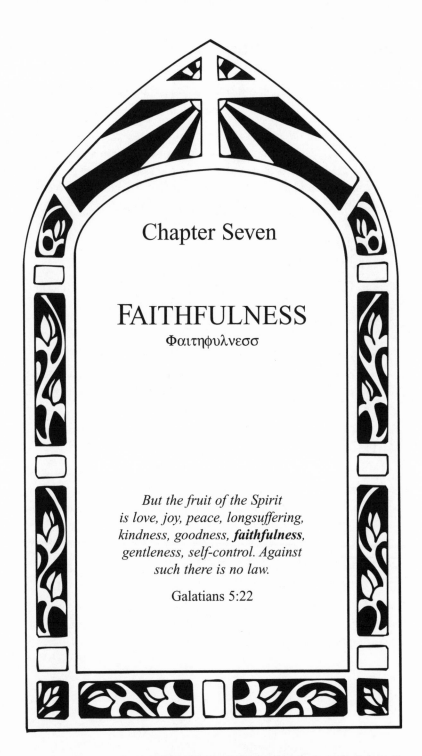

Chapter Seven

FAITHFULNESS

Φαιτηφυλνεσσ

But the fruit of the Spirit
is love, joy, peace, longsuffering,
*kindness, goodness, **faithfulness**,*
gentleness, self-control. Against
such there is no law.

Galatians 5:22

Clement of Rome

First Epistle to the Corinthians

Having then this hope, let our souls be bound to Him who is faithful in His promises, and just in His judgments. – *Chapter 27*

Let a man be faithful: let him be powerful in the utterance of knowledge; let him be wise in judging of words; let him be pure in all his deeds; yet the more he seems to be superior to others in these respects, the more humble-minded ought he to be, and to seek the common good of all, and not merely his own advantage. – *Chapter 48*

Ignatius

Epistle to the Trallians

But the Father of Jesus Christ is faithful to fulfill both mine and your petitions: in whom may we be found without spot. May I have joy of you in the Lord. – *Chapter 13*

Epistle to the Romans

For if I be truly found a Christian, I may also be called one, and be then deemed faithful, when I shall no longer appear to the world. Nothing visible is eternal. – *Chapter 3*

Barnabas

Epistle

Again, and yet again, I beseech you: be good lawgivers to one another; continue faithful counselors of one another; take away from among you all hypocrisy. – *Chapter 21*

Clement of Alexandria

Exhortation to the Heathen

But if, acknowledging the conspicuous trustworthiness of the virtues, you wish to trust them, come and I will set before you in abundance, materials of persuasion respecting the Word. – *Chapter 10*

Instructor Book III

For while it is possible for one who looks to remain steadfast; yet care must be taken against falling. For it is possible for one who looks to slip; but it is impossible for one, who looks not, to lust. For it is not enough for the chaste to be pure; but they must give all diligence, to be beyond the range of censure, shutting out all ground of suspicion, in order to the consummation of chastity; so that we may not only be faithful, but appear worthy of trust. – *Chapter 11*

Stromata Book I

And now the Savior shows Himself, out of His abundance, dispensing goods to His servants according to the ability of the recipient, that they may augment them by exercising activity, and then returning to reckon with them; when, approving of those that had increased His money, those faithful in little, and commanding them to have the charge over many things, He bade them enter into the joy of the Lord. – *Chapter 1*

It is in your power not to be a son of disobedience, but to pass from darkness to life, and lending your ear to wisdom, to be the legal slave of God, in the first instance, and then to become a faithful servant, fearing the Lord God. And if one ascend higher, he is enrolled among the sons. – *Chapter 27*

Stromata Book II

Now he is faithful who keeps inviolably what is entrusted to him; and we are entrusted with the utterances respecting God and the divine words, the commands along with the execution of the injunctions. This is the faithful servant, who is praised by the Lord. – *Chapter 6*

Now His Word declares; and "God" Himself is "faithful." How, then, if to believe is to suppose, do the philosophers think that what proceeds from themselves is sure? For the voluntary assent to a preceding demonstration is not supposition, but it is assent to something sure. – *Chapter 6*

Stromata Book IV

But the faithful is called both servant and friend. So that if one loves himself, he loves the Lord, and confesses to salvation that he may save his soul. – *Chapter 7*

Accordingly, both the old man, the young, and the servant will live faithfully, and if need be die; which will be to be made alive by death. – *Chapter 8*

Stromata Book VI

And who shall understand a parable of the Lord, but the wise, the intelligent, and he that loves his Lord? Let such a man be faithful; let him be capable of uttering his knowledge; let him be wise in the discrimination of words; let him be dexterous in action; let him be pure. – *Chapter 8*

And through the trustworthiness of Him who has promised, he has firmly laid hold of the end of the promise by knowledge. And he, who knows the sure comprehension of the future which there is in the circumstances, in which he is placed, by love goes to meet the future. – *Chapter 9*

Wherefore also man is said to have been made on the sixth day, who became faithful to Him who is the sign, so as straightway to receive the rest of the Lord's inheritance. – *Chapter 16*

Stromata Book VII

Wherefore also all men are His; some through knowledge, and others not yet so; and some as friends, some as faithful servants, some as servants merely. – *Chapter 2*

He must consequently learn to be faithful both to himself and his neighbors, and obedient to the commandments. For he is the true servant of God who spontaneously subjects himself to His commands. – *Chapter 3*

And he who on fitting considerations readily receives and keeps the commandments, is faithful; and he who by love requites benefits as far as he is able, is already a friend. – *Chapter 3*

For every being destined to believe is already faithful in the sight of God, and set up for His honor, an image, endowed with virtue, dedicated to God. – *Chapter 5*

For how can he, that is once faithful, show himself unfaithful, so as to require an oath; and so that his life may not be a sure and decisive oath? He lives, and walks, and shows the trustworthiness of his affirmation in an unwavering and sure life and speech. – *Chapter 8*

For it is not in supposition or seeming that he wishes to be faithful; but in knowledge and truth, that is, in sure deed and effectual word. – *Chapter 11*

So he, who has spurned the ecclesiastical tradition, and darted off to the opinions of heretical men, has ceased to be a man of God and to remain faithful to the Lord. – *Chapter 16*

He, then, who of himself believes the Scripture and voice of the Lord, which by the Lord acts to the benefiting of men, is rightly regarded faithful. – *Chapter 16*

Who Is the Rich Man That Shall Be Saved?

He then is truly and rightly rich who is rich in virtue, and is capable of making a holy and faithful use of any fortune. – *Chapter 19*

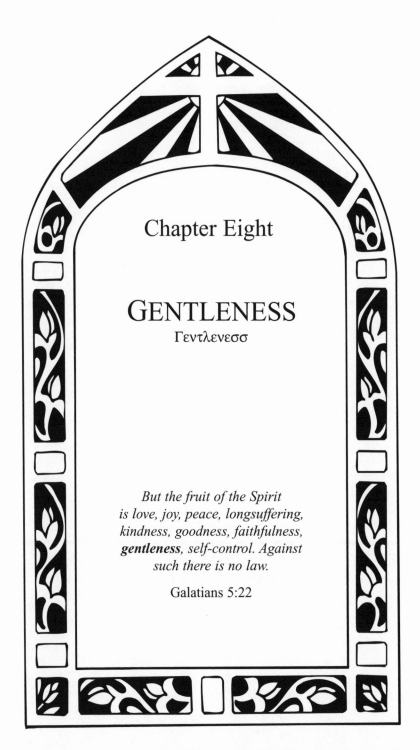

Chapter Eight

GENTLENESS

Γεντλενεσσ

But the fruit of the Spirit
is love, joy, peace, longsuffering,
kindness, goodness, faithfulness,
***gentleness**, self-control. Against*
such there is no law.

Galatians 5:22

Clement of Rome

First Epistle to the Corinthians

Boldness, and arrogance, and audacity belong to those that are accursed of God; but moderation, humility, and meekness to such as are blessed by Him. – *Chapter 30*

Let us then also pray for those who have fallen into any sin, that meekness and humility may be given to them, so that they may submit, not unto us, but to the will of God. – *Chapter 56*

Ignatius

Epistle to the Ephesians

Be ye meek in response to their wrath, humble in opposition to their boasting: to their blasphemies return your prayers; in contrast to their error, be ye steadfast in the faith; and for their cruelty, manifest your gentleness. – *Chapter 10*

Conquer ye their harsh temper by gentleness, their passion by meekness. – *Chapter 10*

Epistle to the Trallians

I therefore have need of meekness, by which the devil, the prince of this world, is brought to naught. – *Chapter 4*

Wherefore, clothing yourselves with meekness, be ye renewed in faith, that is the flesh of the Lord, and in love, that is the blood of Jesus Christ. – *Chapter 8*

Epistle to the Philadelphians

For they are not Christ's husbandry, but the seed of the enemy, from whom may you ever be delivered by the prayers of the shepherd, that most faithful and gentle shepherd who presides over you. – *Chapter 3*

Masters, be gentle towards your servants, as holy Job has taught you; for there is one nature, and one family of mankind. – *Chapter 4*

Epistle to Polycarp

If thou lovest the good disciples only, thou hast no grace; but rather subdue those that are evil by gentleness. All sorts of wounds are not healed by the same medicine. Mitigate the pain of cutting by tenderness. Be wise as the serpent in everything, and innocent, with respect to those things which are requisite, even as the dove. – *Chapter 2*

Second Epistle to the Ephesians

Against their harsh words be ye conciliatory, by meekness of mind and gentleness. – *Chapter 10*

Barnabas

Epistle

Thou shalt be meek: thou shalt be peaceable. – *Chapter 19*

Justin Martyr

First Apology

For we ought not to strive; neither has He desired us to be imitators of wicked men, but He has exhorted us to lead all men, by patience and gentleness, from shame and the love of evil. – *Chapter 16*

Dialogue with Trypho, A Jew

Press on in Thy fairness and in Thy beauty, and prosper and reign, because of truth, and of meekness, and of righteousness: and Thy right hand shall instruct Thee marvelously. – *Chapter 38*

Irenaeus

Against Heresies Book IV

For by such means was the prophet—very indignant, because of the transgression of the people and the slaughter of the prophets—both taught to act in a more gentle manner; and the Lord's advent as a man was pointed out, that it should be subsequent to that law which was given by Moses, mild and tranquil, in which He would neither break the bruised reed, nor quench the smoking flax. – *Chapter 20*

For, after the wind which rends the mountains, and after the earthquake, and after the fire, come the tranquil and peaceful times of His kingdom, in which the spirit of God does, in the most gentle manner, vivify and increase mankind. – *Chapter 20*

Hermas

Pastor Book II

The tender Spirit, then, not being accustomed to dwell with the wicked spirit, nor with hardness, withdraws from such a man, and seeks to dwell with meekness and peacefulness. – *Commandment 5, Chapter 2*

The angel of righteousness is gentle and modest, meek and peaceful. When, therefore, he ascends into your heart, forthwith he talks to you of righteousness, purity, chastity, contentment, and of every righteous deed and glorious virtue. When all these ascend into your heart, know that the angel of righteousness is with you. – *Commandment 6, Chapter 2*

You will practice righteousness and virtue, truth and the fear of the Lord, faith and meekness, and whatsoever excellences are like to these. Practicing these, you will be a well-pleasing servant of God, and you will live to Him; and every one who shall serve good desire, shall live to God. – *Commandment 12, Chapter 3*

Pastor Book III

The Lord, therefore, seeing their simplicity and all their meekness, multiplied them amid the labors of their hands, and gave them grace in all their doings. – *Similitude 9, Chapter 24*

Theophilus of Antioch

To Autolycus Book II

When, therefore, man again shall have made his way back to his natural condition, and no longer does evil, those also shall be restored to their original gentleness. – *Chapter 17*

Athenagoras

A Plea for the Christians

But, because we are persuaded that we shall give an account of everything in the present life to God, who made us and the world, we adopt a temperate and benevolent and generally despised method of life, believing that we shall suffer no such great evil here, even should our lives be taken from us, compared with what we shall there receive for our meek and benevolent and moderate life from the great Judge. – *Chapter 12*

Clement of Alexandria

Instructor Book I

The Pedagogue strengthening our souls, and by His benign commands, as by gentle medicines, guiding the sick to the perfect knowledge of the truth. – *Chapter 1*

The child is therefore gentle, and therefore more tender, delicate, and simple, guileless, and destitute of hypocrisy, straightforward and upright in mind, which is the basis of simplicity and truth. – *Chapter 5*

Thus also the Father of the universe cherishes affection towards those who have fled to Him; and having begotten them again by His Spirit to the adoption of children, knows them as gentle, and loves those alone, and aids and fights for them; and therefore He bestows on them the name of child. – *Chapter 5*

Instructor Book III

A true gentleman must have no mark of effeminacy visible on his face, or any other part of his body. – *Chapter 11*

Such ought those who are consecrated to Christ appear, and frame themselves in their whole life, as they fashion themselves in the church for the sake of gravity; and to be, not to seem such—so meek, so pious, so loving. – *Chapter 11*

When the kingdom is worthily tested, we dispense the affection of the soul by a chaste and closed mouth, by which chiefly gentle manners are expressed. – *Chapter 11*

Stromata Book I

For nutriment, and the training which is maintained gentle, make noble natures. – *Chapter 6*

Stromata Book II

For God, the author and the dispenser of such grace, takes as suitable usury the most precious things to be found among men—mildness, gentleness, magnanimity, reputation, renown. – *Chapter 18*

Now love is conceived in many ways, in the form of meekness, of mildness, of patience, of liberality, of freedom from envy, of absence of hatred, of forgetfulness of injuries. In all it is incapable of being divided or distinguished: its nature is to communicate. – *Chapter 18*

Stromata Book IV

And the meek are those who have quelled the battle of unbelief in the soul, the battle of wrath, and lust, and the other forms that are subject to them. And He praises those meek by choice, not by necessity. – *Chapter 6*

Let them manifest the gentleness of their tongue by silence. – *Chapter 17*

Stromata Book VI

For the Almighty God, in His care for all men, turns some to salvation by commands, some by threats, some by miraculous signs, some by gentle promises. – *Chapter 3*

For he who is convened from among the Gentiles is formed from a beastlike life to gentleness by the word; and, when once tamed, is made clean, just as the ox. – *Chapter 6*

Chapter Nine

SELF-CONTROL

Σελφ–Χοντρολ

But the fruit of the Spirit
is love, joy, peace, longsuffering,
kindness, goodness, faithfulness,
*gentleness, **self-control**. Against*
such there is no law.

Galatians 5:22

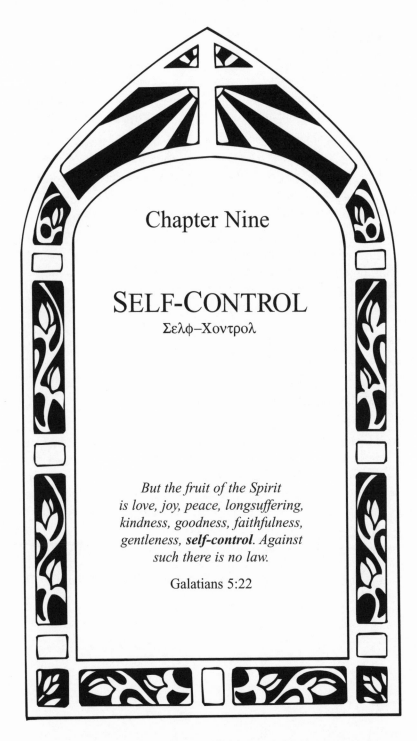

Clement of Rome

First Epistle to the Corinthians

Let us clothe ourselves with concord and humility, ever exercising self-control, standing far off from all whispering and evil-speaking, being justified by our works, and not our words. – *Chapter 30*

How blessed and wonderful, beloved, are the gifts of God! Life in immortality, splendor in righteousness, truth in perfect confidence, faith in assurance, self-control in holiness! And all these fall under the cognizance of our understandings now; what then shall those things be which are prepared for such as wait for Him? – *Chapter 35*

May God, who seeth all things, and who is the Ruler of all spirits and the Lord of all flesh—who chose our Lord Jesus Christ and us through Him to be a peculiar people—grant to every soul that calleth upon His glorious and holy Name, faith, fear, peace, patience, longsuffering, self-control, purity, and sobriety, to the well-pleasing of His Name, through our High Priest and Protector, Jesus Christ, by whom be to Him glory, and majesty, and power, and honor, both now and forevermore. Amen. – *Chapter 58*

Justin Martyr

First Apology

And we have been taught, and are convinced, and do believe, that He accepts those only who imitate the excellences which reside in Him, temperance, and justice, and philanthropy, and as many virtues as are peculiar to a God who is called by no proper name. And we have been taught that He in the beginning did of His goodness, for man's sake, create all things out of unformed matter; and if men by their works show themselves worthy of this His design, they are deemed worthy, and so we have received—of reigning in company with Him, being delivered from corruption and suffering. – *Chapter 10*

Irenaeus

Against Heresies Book III

God does, however, exercise a providence over all things, and therefore He also gives counsel; and when giving counsel, He is present with those who attend to moral discipline. – *Chapter 25*

Hermas

Pastor Book I

But you are saved, because you did not depart from the living God, and on account of your simplicity and great self-control. These have saved you, if you remain steadfast. And they will save all who act in the same manner, and walk in guilelessness and simplicity. – *Chapter 3*

For from faith arises self-restraint; from self-restraint, simplicity; from simplicity, guilelessness; from guilelessness, chastity; from chastity, intelligence; and from intelligence, love. The deeds, then, of these are pure, and chaste, and divine. Whoever devotes himself to these, and is able to hold fast by their works, shall have his dwelling in the tower with the saints of God. – *Chapter 8*

Pastor Book II

Have faith therefore in Him, and fear Him; and fearing Him, exercise self-control. Keep these commands, and you will cast away from you all wickedness, and put on the strength of righteousness, and live to God, if you keep this commandment. – *Commandment 1*

Theophilus of Antioch

To Autolycus Book III

But far be it from Christians to conceive any such deeds; for with them temperance dwells, self-restraint is practiced, monogamy is observed, chastity is guarded, iniquity exterminated, sin extirpated, righteousness exercised, law administered, worship performed, God acknowledged: truth governs, grace guards, peace screens them; the holy word guides, wisdom teaches, life directs, God reigns. – *Chapter 15*

Athenagoras

A Plea for the Christians

Those, then, who are forbidden to look at anything more than that for which God formed the eyes, which were intended to be a light to us, and to whom a wanton look is adultery, the eyes being made for other purposes, and who are to be called to account for their very thoughts, how can any one doubt that such persons practice self-control? – *Chapter 32*

Clement of Alexandria

Instructor Book I

For if the God of both is one, the master of both is also one; one church, one temperance, one modesty; their food is common, marriage an equal yoke; respiration, sight, hearing, knowledge, hope, obedience, love all alike. – *Chapter 4*

For this is the medicine of the divine love to man, by which the blush of modesty breaks forth, and shame at sin supervenes. For if one must censure, it is necessary also to rebuke; when it is the time to wound the apathetic soul not mortally, but salutarily, securing exemption from everlasting death by a little pain. – *Chapter 8*

For reproof and rebuke, as also the original term implies, are the stripes of the soul, chastising sins, preventing death, and leading to self-control those carried away to licentiousness. – *Chapter 9*

Instructor Book II

And just as righteousness is not attained by avarice, nor temperance by excess; so neither is the regimen of a Christian formed by indulgence; for the table of truth is far from lascivious dainties. – *Chapter 1*

I therefore admire those who have adopted an austere life, and who are fond of water, the medicine of temperance, and flee as far as possible from wine, shunning it as they would the danger of fire. – *Chapter 2*

For being moored by reason and time, as by anchors, they stand with greater ease the storm of passions which rushes down from intemperance. – *Chapter 2*

For nothing disgraceful is proper for man, who is endowed with reason; much less for woman, to whom it brings modesty even to reflect of what nature she is. – *Chapter 2*

Let temperance raise us as from the abyss beneath to the enterprises of wakefulness. – *Chapter 9*

For, lo, this mortal shall put on immortality; when the insatiableness of desire, which rushes into licentiousness, being trained to self-restraint, and made free from the love of corruption, shall consign the man to everlasting chastity. – *Chapter 10*

And excellence alone appears through the beautiful body, and blossoms out in the flesh, exhibiting the amiable comeliness of self-control, whenever the character like a beam of light gleams in the form. – *Chapter 13*

And the excellence of man is righteousness, and temperance, and manliness, and godliness. The beautiful man is, then, he who is just, temperate, and in a word, good, not he who is rich. – *Chapter 13*

Instructor Book III

This is the Word, who abjures luxury, but calls self-help as a servant, and praises frugality, the progeny of temperance. – *Chapter 6*

Temperance is pure and simple; since purity is a habit which ensures pure conduct unmixed with what is base. Simplicity is a habit which does away with superfluities. – *Chapter 11*

But temperance in drinks, and moderation in articles of food, are effectual in producing beauty according to nature; for not only does the body maintain its health from these, but they also make beauty to appear. – *Chapter 11*

Stromata Book II

With temperance also is conjoined caution, which is avoidance in accordance with reason. – *Chapter 18*

Self-restraint is that quality which does not overstep what appears in accordance with right reason. He exercises self-restraint, who curbs the impulses that are contrary to right reason, or curbs himself so as not to indulge in desires contrary to right reason. – *Chapter 18*

For the good man, standing as the boundary between an immortal and a mortal nature, has few needs; having wants in consequence of his body, and his birth itself, but taught by rational self-control to want few things. – *Chapter 18*

Stromata Book IV

For self-control is common to all human beings who have made choice of it. And we admit that the same nature exists in every race, and the same virtue. – *Chapter 8*

In the contemplative life, then, one in worshipping God attends to himself, and through his own spotless purification beholds the holy God holily; for self-control, being present, surveying and contemplating itself uninterruptedly, is as far as possible assimilated to God. – *Chapter 23*

Stromata Book VI

Knowledge is then followed by practical wisdom, and practical wisdom by self-control: for it may be said that practical wisdom is divine knowledge, and exists in those who are deified; but that self-control is mortal, and subsists in those who philosophize, and are not yet wise. But if virtue is divine, so is also the knowledge of it; while self-control is a sort of imperfect wisdom which aspires after wisdom, and exerts itself laboriously, and is not contemplative. – *Chapter 15*

Stromata Book VII

Then by the practice of temperance men seek health: and by cramming themselves, and wallowing in potations at feasts, they attract diseases. – *Chapter 4*

And the same holds with self-control. For it is neither for love of honor, as the athletes for the sake of crowns and fame; nor on the other hand, for love of money, as some pretend to exercise self-control, pursuing what is good with terrible suffering. Nor is it from love of the body for the sake of health. Nor any more is any man who is temperate from rusticity, who has not tasted pleasures, truly a man of self-control. – *Chapter 11*

But self-control, desirable for its own sake, perfected through knowledge, abiding ever, makes the man lord and master of himself. – *Chapter 11*

Chapter Ten

RIGHTEOUSNESS

Ριγητεουσνεσσ

*For you were once darkness, but now you are light in the Lord. Walk as children of light (for the fruit of the Spirit is in all goodness, **righteousness**, and truth), finding out what is acceptable to the Lord.*

Ephesians 5:8-10

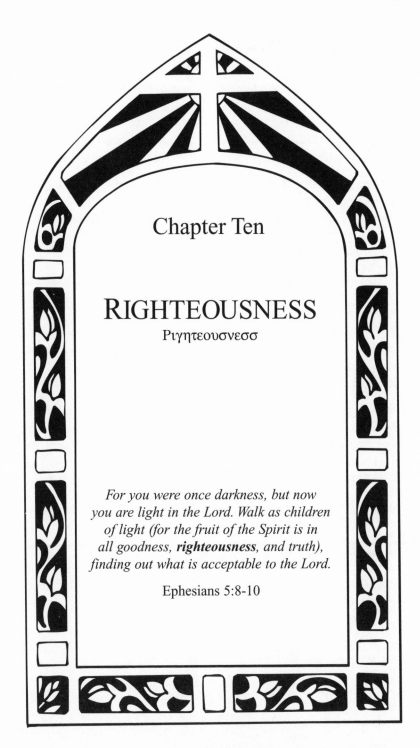

Clement of Rome

First Epistle to the Corinthians

Let us cleave then to His blessing, and consider what are the means of possessing it. Let us think over the things which have taken place from the beginning. For what reason was our father Abraham blessed? Was it not because he wrought righteousness and truth through faith? – *Chapter 31*

We see, then, how all righteous men have been adorned with good works, and how the Lord Himself, adorning Himself with His works, rejoiced. Having therefore such an example, let us without delay accede to His will, and let us work the work of righteousness with our whole strength. – *Chapter 33*

If our understanding be fixed by faith rewards God; if we earnestly seek the things which are pleasing and acceptable to Him; if we do the things which are in harmony with His blameless will; and if we follow the way of truth, casting away from us all unrighteousness and iniquity, along with all covetousness, strife, evil practices, deceit, whispering, and evil-speaking, all hatred of God, pride and haughtiness, vainglory and ambition. – *Chapter 35*

Look carefully into the Scriptures, which are the true utterances of the Holy Spirit. Observe that nothing of an unjust or counterfeit character is written in them. There you will not find that the righteous were cast off by men who themselves were holy. The righteous were indeed persecuted, but only by the wicked. – *Chapter 45*

Let us cleave, therefore, to the innocent and righteous, since these are the elect of God. (Chapter 46)

Many gates have been set open, yet this gate of righteousness is that gate in Christ by which blessed are all they that have entered in and have directed their way in holiness and righteousness, doing all things without disorder. – *Chapter 48*

Mathetes

Epistle to Diognetus

For what other thing was capable of covering our sins than His righteousness? By what other one was it possible that we, the wicked and ungodly, could be justified, than by the only Son of God? – *Chapter 9*

Polycarp

Epistle to the Philippians

Let us arm ourselves with the armor of righteousness; and let us teach, first of all, ourselves to walk in the commandments of the Lord. – *Chapter 4*

In like manner should the deacons be blameless before the face of His righteousness, as being the servants of God and Christ, and not of men. – *Chapter 5*

I exhort you all, therefore, to yield obedience to the word of righteousness, and to exercise all patience, such as ye have seen set before your eyes, not only in the case of the blessed Ignatius, and Zosimus, and Rufus, but also in others among yourselves, and in Paul himself, and the rest of the apostles. This do in the assurance that all these have not run in vain, but in faith and righteousness, and that they are now in their due place in the presence of the Lord, with whom also they suffered. – *Chapter 9*

Ignatius

Epistle to the Ephesians

What communion hath truth with falsehood? or righteousness with unrighteousness? or true doctrine with that which is false? – *Chapter 16*

Barnabas

Epistle

Seeing that the divine fruits of righteousness abound among you, I rejoice exceedingly and above measure in your happy and honored spirits, because ye have with such effect received the engrafted spiritual gift. – *Chapter 1*

Then shall thy dawn break forth, and thy healing shall quickly spring up, and righteousness shall go forth before thee, and the glory of God shall encompass thee; and then thou shalt call, and God shall hear thee. – *Chapter 3*

The Lord will judge the world without respect of persons. Each will receive as he has done: if he is righteous, his righteousness will precede him; if he is wicked, the reward of wickedness is before him. – *Chapter 4*

The man perishes justly, who, having a knowledge of the way of righteousness, rushes off into the way of darkness. – *Chapter 5*

Behold, therefore: certainly then one properly resting sanctifies it, when we ourselves, having received the promise, wickedness no longer existing, and all things having been made new by the Lord, shall be able to work righteousness. – *Chapter 15*

Thou shalt not be joined in soul with the haughty, but thou shalt be reckoned with the righteous and lowly. – *Chapter 19*

Thou shalt judge righteously. – *Chapter 19*

Justin Martyr

Dialogue with Trypho, a Jew

Let the wicked forsake his ways, and the unrighteous man his thoughts; and let him return unto the Lord, and he will obtain mercy, because He will abundantly pardon your sins. – *Chapter 14*

Loose every unrighteous bond, dissolve the terms of wrongous covenants, let the oppressed go free, and avoid every iniquitous contract. – *Chapter 15*

Then shall thy light break forth as the morning, and thy garments shall rise up quickly: and thy righteousness shall go before thee, and the glory of God shall envelope thee. – *Chapter 15*

Moreover, all those righteous men already mentioned, though they kept no Sabbaths, were pleasing to God. – *Chapter 19*

But let judgment be rolled down as water, and righteousness as an impassable torrent. – *Chapter 22*

Moreover, the Scriptures and the facts themselves compel us to admit that He received circumcision for a sign, and not for righteousness. – *Chapter 33*

And, furthermore, the inability of the female sex to receive fleshly circumcision, proves that this circumcision has been given for a sign, and not for a work of righteousness. – *Chapter 33*

But neither shall the father perish for the son, nor the son for the father; but every one for his own sin, and each shall be saved for his own righteousness. – *Chapter 140*

Fragments

The greatest of all good is to be free from sin, the next is to be justified; but he must be reckoned the most unfortunate of men, who, while living unrighteously, remains for a long time unpunished. – *Chapter 18*

Irenaeus

Against Heresies Book I

For men are saved through his grace, and not on account of their own righteous actions. For such deeds are not righteous in the nature of things, but by mere accident, just as those angels who made the world, have thought fit to constitute them, seeking, by means of such precepts, to bring men into bondage. – *Chapter 23*

Against Heresies Book II

And the righteous suffer persecution, are afflicted, and are slain, while sinners are possessed of abundance, and "drink with the sound of the harp and psaltery, but do not regard the works of the Lord." – *Chapter 22*

Against Heresies Book III

And they do please God, ordering their conversation in all righteousness, chastity, and wisdom. – *Chapter 4*

For as by one man's disobedience sin entered, and death obtained a place through sin; so also by the obedience of one man, righteousness having been introduced, shall cause life to fructify in those persons who in times past were dead. – *Chapter 21*

Against Heresies Book IV

Righteously also the apostles, being of the race of Abraham, left the ship and their father, and followed the Word. Righteously also do we, possessing the same faith as Abraham, and taking up the cross as Isaac did the wood, follow Him. – *Chapter 5*

For all the righteous possess the sacerdotal rank. And all the apostles of the Lord are priests, who do inherit here neither lands nor houses, but serve God and the altar continually. – *Chapter 8*

Moreover, we learn from the Scripture itself, that God gave circumcision, not as the completer of righteousness, but as a sign, that the race of Abraham might continue recognizable. – *Chapter 16*

But the righteous fathers had the meaning of the Decalogue written in their hearts and souls, that is, they loved the God who made them, and did no injury to their neighbor. – *Chapter 16*

For the Church alone sustains with purity the reproach of those who suffer persecution for righteousness' sake, and endure all sorts of punishments, and are put to death because of the love which they bear to God, and their confession of His Son. – *Chapter 33*

Against Heresies Book V

Those, then, are the perfect who have had the Spirit of God remaining in them, and have preserved their souls and bodies blameless, holding fast the faith of God, that is, that faith which is directed towards God, and maintaining righteous dealings with respect to their neighbors. – *Chapter 6*

Hermas

Pastor Book I

You will tell, therefore, those who preside over the Church, to direct their ways in righteousness, that they may receive in full the promises with great glory. Stand steadfast, therefore, ye who work righteousness, and doubt not, that your passage may be with the holy angels. – *Vision 2, Chapter 2*

Pastor Book II

Have faith therefore in Him, and fear Him; and fearing Him, exercise self-control. Keep these commands, and you will cast away from you all wickedness, and put on the strength of righteousness, and live to God, if you keep this commandment. – *Commandment 1*

Trust you, therefore, the righteous, but put no trust in the unrighteous. For the path of righteousness is straight, but that of unrighteousness is crooked. – *Commandment 6, Chapter 1*

Even as beautiful vines, when they are neglected, are withered up by thorns and divers plants, so men who have believed, and have afterwards fallen away into many of those actions above mentioned, go astray in their minds, and lose all understanding in regard to righteousness; for if they hear of righteousness, their minds are occupied with their business, and they give no heed at all. – *Commandment 10, Chapter 1*

You must refrain from evil desires, that by refraining ye may live to God. But as many as are mastered by them, and do not resist them, will perish at last, for these desires are fatal. Put you on, then, the desire of righteousness; and arming yourself with the fear of the Lord, resist them. For the fear of the Lord dwells in good desire. – *Commandment 12, Chapter 2*

Theophilus of Antioch

To Autolycus Book II

So also the world, if it had not had the law of God and the prophets flowing and welling up sweetness, and compassion, and righteousness, and the doctrine of the holy commandments of God, would long ere now have come to ruin, by reason of the wickedness and sin which abound in it. – *Chapter 14*

But all these things will every one understand who seeks the wisdom of God, and is well pleasing to Him through faith and righteousness and the doing of good works. – *Chapter 38*

Clement of Alexandria

Exhortation to the Heathen

What, then, does this instrument—the Word of God, the Lord, the New Song—desire? To open the eyes of the blind, and unstop the ears of the deaf, and to lead the lame or the erring to righteousness, to exhibit God to the foolish, to put a stop to corruption, to conquer death, to reconcile disobedient children to their father. The instrument of God loves mankind. – *Chapter 1*

Let us therefore repent, and pass from ignorance to knowledge, from foolishness to wisdom, from licentiousness to self-restraint, from unrighteousness to righteousness, from godlessness to God. It is an enterprise of noble daring to take our way to God; and the enjoyment of many other good things is within the reach of the lovers of righteousness, who pursue eternal life. – *Chapter 10*

For he that is fired with ardor and admiration for righteousness, being the lover of One who needs nothing, needs himself but little, having treasured up his bliss in nothing but himself and God, where is neither moth, robber, nor pirate, but the eternal Giver of good. – *Chapter 10*

This is the proclamation of righteousness: to those that obey, glad tidings; to those that disobey, judgment. – *Chapter 11*

Instructor Book I

Feed us, the children, as sheep. Yea, Master, fill us with righteousness, Thine own pasture; yea, O Instructor, feed us on Thy holy mountain the Church, which towers aloft, which is above the clouds, which touches heaven. – *Chapter 9*

Instructor Book II

That fish then which, at the command of the Lord, Peter caught, points to digestible and God-given and moderate food. And by those who rise from the water to the bait of righteousness, He admonishes us to take away luxury and avarice, as the coin from the fish; in order that He might displace vainglory. – *Chapter 1*

Manly He calls those who despise wealth, and are free in bestowing it. And on your feet let active readiness to well-doing appear, and a journeying to righteousness. Modesty and chastity are collars and necklaces; such are the chains which God forges. – *Chapter 13*

Instructor Book III

Accordingly, good things are possessed by Christians alone. And nothing is richer than these good things; therefore these alone are rich. For righteousness is true riches; and the Word is more valuable than all treasure, not accruing from cattle and fields, but given by God—riches which cannot be taken away. – *Chapter 6*

Stromata Book II

For a man is made to communicate by righteousness, and bestows what he received from God, in consequence of his natural benevolence and relation, and the commands which he obeys. – *Chapter 16*

Temperance, too, is not without manliness; since from the commandments spring both wisdom, which follows God who enjoins, and that which imitates the divine character, namely righteousness; in virtue of which, in the exercise of self-restraint, we address ourselves in purity to piety and the course of conduct thence resulting, in conformity with God; being assimilated to the Lord as far as is possible for us beings mortal in nature. – *Chapter 18*

Stromata Book IV

He clearly taught us in every circumstance to seek for the martyr who, if poor for righteousness' sake, witnesses that the righteousness which he loves is a good thing; and if he "hunger and thirst for righteousness' sake," testifies that righteousness is the best thing. Likewise he, that weeps and mourns for righteousness' sake, testifies to the best law that it is beautiful. – *Chapter 6*

It is not the poor simply, but those that have wished to become poor for righteousness' sake, that He pronounces blessed—those who have despised the honors of this world in order to attain "the good." – *Chapter 6*

But our true "treasure" is where what is allied to our mind is, since it bestows the communicative power of righteousness, showing that we must assign to the habit of our old conversation what we have acquired by it, and have recourse to God, beseeching mercy. – *Chapter 6*

Accordingly woman is to practice self-restraint and righteousness, and every other virtue, as well as man, both bond and free; since it is a fit consequence that the same nature possesses one and the same virtue. – *Chapter 8*

Accordingly, they unwillingly bear testimony to our righteousness, we being unjustly punished for righteousness' sake. But the injustice of the judge does not affect the providence of God. – *Chapter 11*

Such being the case, the prophets are perfect in prophecy, the righteous in righteousness, and the martyrs in confession, and others in preaching, not that they are not sharers in the common virtues, but are proficient in those to which they are appointed. – *Chapter 21*

But the apostles were perfected in all. You will find, then, if you choose, in their acts and writings, knowledge, life, preaching, righteousness, purity, prophecy. – *Chapter 21*

This is in reality righteousness, not to desire other things, but to be entirely the consecrated temple of the Lord. – *Chapter 25*

For wisdom is the knowledge of things divine and human; and righteousness is the concord of the parts of the soul; and holiness is the service of God. – *Chapter 26*

Stromata Book VI

And in whomsoever the increased force of righteousness advances to the doing of good, in his case perfection abides in the fixed habit of well-doing after the likeness of God. – *Chapter 7*

As appears, then, righteousness is quadrangular; on all sides equal and like in word, in deed, in abstinence from evils, in beneficence, in gnostic perfection; nowhere, and in no respect halting, so that he does not appear unjust and unequal. As one, then, is righteous, so certainly is he a believer. But as he is a believer, he is not yet also righteous—I mean according to the righteousness of progress and perfection, according to which the Gnostic is called righteous. – *Chapter 12*

Not only then the believer, but even the heathen, is judged most righteously. – *Chapter 14*

And giving thanks always for all things to God, by righteous hearing and divine reading, by true investigation, by holy oblation, by blessed prayer; lauding, hymning, blessing, praising, such a soul is never at any time separated from God. – *Chapter 14*

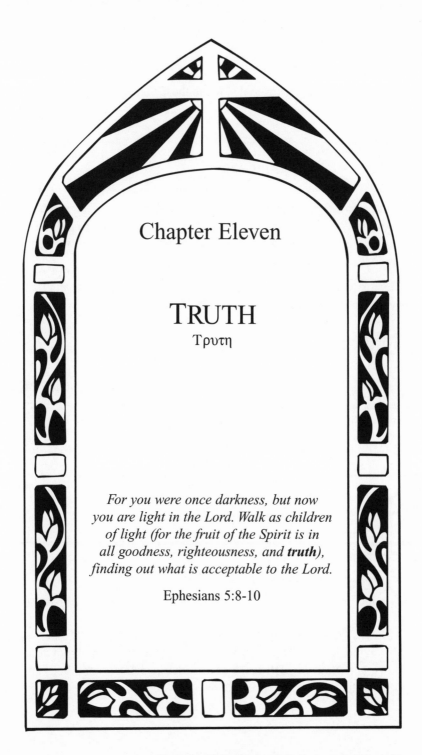

Chapter Eleven

TRUTH

Τρυτη

For you were once darkness, but now you are light in the Lord. Walk as children of light (for the fruit of the Spirit is in all goodness, righteousness, and ***truth****), finding out what is acceptable to the Lord.*

Ephesians 5:8-10

Mathetes

Epistle to Diognetus

I minister the things delivered to me to those that are disciples worthy of the truth. – *Chapter 11*

Polycarp

Epistle to the Philippians

Stand fast, therefore, in these things, and follow the example of the Lord, being firm and unchangeable in the faith, loving the brotherhood, and being attached to one another, joined together in the truth, exhibiting the meekness of the Lord in your intercourse with one another, and despising no one. – *Chapter 10*

I exhort you, therefore, that ye abstain from covetousness, and that ye be chaste and truthful. – *Chapter 11*

Ignatius

Epistle to the Ephesians

In like manner, every one that has received from God the power of distinguishing, and yet follows an unskillful shepherd, and receives a false opinion for the truth, shall be punished. – *Chapter 16*

Why do we foolishly perish, not recognizing the gift which the Lord has of a truth sent to us? – *Chapter 17*

Epistle to the Magnesians

The believing possess the image of their Prince, God the Father, and Jesus Christ, through whom, if we are not in readiness to die for the truth into His passion, His life is not in us. – *Chapter 5*

Epistle to the Trallians

For that which is false is quite abhorrent to the truth. – *Chapter 10*

Epistle to the Philadelphians

Wherefore, as children of light and truth, avoid the dividing of your unity, and the wicked doctrine of the doctrines; but where the shepherd is, there do ye as sheep follow. – *Chapter 2*

If any man follows him that separates from the truth, he shall not inherit the kingdom of God; and if any man does not stand aloof from the preacher of falsehood, he shall be condemned to hell. – *Chapter 3*

Epistle to the Smyrnaeans

Some have ignorantly denied Him, and advocate falsehood rather than the truth. – *Chapter 5*

Epistle to Polycarp

Let not those who seem to be somewhat, and teach strange doctrines, strike thee with apprehension; but stand thou in the truth, as an athlete who is smitten, for it is the part of a great athlete to be smitten, and yet conquer. – *Chapter 3*

Justin Martyr

First Apology

It is incumbent on the lover of truth, by all means, and if death be threatened, even before his own life, to choose to do and say what is right. – *Chapter 2*

In the beginning He made the human race with the power of thought and of choosing the truth and doing right, so that all men are without excuse before God; for they have been born rational and contemplative. – *Chapter 28*

So many things therefore, as these, when they are seen with the eye, are enough to produce conviction and belief in those who embrace the truth, and are not bigoted in their opinions, nor are governed by their passions. – *Chapter 53*

On the Resurrection

The word of truth is free, and carries its own authority, disdaining to fall under any skillful argument, or to endure the logical scrutiny of its hearers. – *Chapter 1*

Irenaeus

Against Heresies Book I

But as the sun, that creature of God, is one and the same throughout the whole world, so also the preaching of the truth shineth everywhere, and enlightens all men that are willing to come to a knowledge of the truth. – *Chapter 10*

Against Heresies Book V

For the Church preaches the truth everywhere, and she is the seven-branched candlestick which bears the light of Christ. – *Chapter 20*

Hermas

Pastor Book II

For where the Lord dwells, there is much understanding. Cleave, then, to the Lord, and you will understand and perceive all things. – *Commandment 10, Chapter 1*

Theophilus of Antioch

To Autolycus Book I

The lover of truth does not give heed to ornamented speeches, but examines the real matter of the speech, what it is, and what kind it is. – *Chapter 1*

To Autolycus Book II

In order, therefore, that the truth might be obvious, the plants and seeds were produced prior to the heavenly bodies, for what is posterior cannot produce that which is prior. – *Chapter 15*

And therefore it is proved that all others have been in error; and that we Christians alone have possessed the truth, inasmuch as we are taught by the Holy Spirit, who spoke in the holy prophets, and foretold all things. – *Chapter 33*

For those who desire it, can, by reading what they uttered, accurately understand the truth, and no longer be carried away by opinion and profitless labor. These, then, whom we have already mentioned, were prophets among the Hebrews—illiterate, and shepherds, and uneducated. – *Chapter 35*

Clement of Alexandria

Exhortation to the Heathen

The union of many in one, issuing in the production of divine harmony out of a medley of sounds and division, becomes one symphony following one choir-leader and teacher, the Word, reaching and resting in the same truth, and crying Abba, Father. This, the true utterance of His children, God accepts with gracious welcome—the first-fruits He receives from them. – *Chapter 9*

For, in the name of truth, what man in his senses turns his back on good, and attaches himself to evil? – *Chapter 10*

Thence praise-worthy works descend to us, and fly with us on the wing of truth. – *Chapter 10*

Receive, then, the water of the word; wash, ye polluted ones; purify yourselves from custom, by sprinkling yourselves with the drops of truth. – *Chapter 10*

A noble hymn of God is an immortal man, established in righteousness, in whom the oracles of truth are engraved. – *Chapter 10*

Instructor Book I

For so is the truth, that perfection is with the Lord, who is always teaching, and infancy and childishness with us, who are always learning. – *Chapter 5*

And that which participates in eternity is wont to be assimilated to the incorruptible: so that to us appertains the designation of the age of childhood, a lifelong springtime, because the truth that is in us, and our habits saturated with the truth, cannot be touched by old age; but Wisdom is ever blooming, ever remains consistent and the same, and never changes. – *Chapter 5*

For we drink in the word, the nutriment of the truth. – *Chapter 6*

Now the instruction which is of God is the right direction of truth to the contemplation of God, and the exhibition of holy deeds in everlasting perseverance. – *Chapter 7*

It is clear, then, that those who are not at enmity with the truth, and do not hate the Word, will not hate their own salvation, but will escape the punishment of enmity. – *Chapter 8*

I say, too, that it is requisite to contemplate human nature, and to live as the truth directs, and to admire the Instructor and His injunctions, as suitable and harmonious to each other. According to which image also we ought, conforming ourselves to the Instructor, and making the word and our deeds agree, to live a real life. – *Chapter 12*

And Christian conduct is the operation of the rational soul in accordance with a correct judgment and aspiration after the truth, which attains its destined end through the body, the soul's consort and ally. – *Chapter 13*

Instructor Book III

Therefore, being regenerated, let us fix ourselves to it in truth, and return to sobriety, and sanctify ourselves. – *Chapter 12*

Stromata Book I

And those who have been rightly reared in the words of truth, and received provision for eternal life, wing their way to heaven. – *Chapter 1*

Among many small pearls there is the one; and in a great take of fish there is the beauty-fish; and by time and toil truth will gleam forth, if a good helper is at hand. For most benefits are supplied, from God, through men. – *Chapter 1*

Stromata Book IV

Now, to disbelieve truth brings death, as to believe, life; and again, to believe the lie and to disbelieve the truth hurries to destruction. – *Chapter 3*

For blessed is he who shall do and teach the Lord's commands worthily; and he is of a magnanimous mind, and of a mind contemplative of truth. – *Chapter 17*

Stromata Book V

Wise souls, pure as virgins, understanding themselves to be situated amidst the ignorance of the world, kindle the light, and rouse the mind, and illumine the darkness, and dispel ignorance, and seek truth, and await the appearance of the Teacher. – *Chapter 3*

For the many demand demonstration as a pledge of truth, not satisfied with the bare salvation by faith. – *Chapter 3*

Men must then be saved by learning the truth through Christ, even if they attain philosophy. – *Chapter 13*

He, then, who is not obedient to the truth, and is puffed up with human teaching, is wretched and miserable. – *Chapter 14*

Stromata Book VI

You see whence the true philosophy has its handles; though the Law be the image and shadow of the truth: for the Law is the shadow of the truth. – *Chapter 7*

For the light of truth—a light true, casting no shadow, is the Spirit of God indivisibly divided to all, who are sanctified by faith, holding the place of a luminary, in order to the knowledge of real existences. By following Him, therefore, through our whole life, we become impassible; and this is to rest. – *Chapter 16, Commandment 4*

Truth is not taught by imitation, but by instruction. – *Chapter 17*

Stromata Book VII

Thus also it appears to me that there are three effects of gnostic power: the knowledge of things; second, the performance of whatever the Word suggests; and the third, the capability of delivering, in a way suitable to God, the secrets veiled in the truth. – *Chapter 1*

About the Editor

GEORGE D. ZGOURIDES, Psy.D., is a clinical psychologist and Orthodox priest specializing in mind-body-spirit psychology with a focus on health. Dr. Zgourides has written a number of books that include *Stop Feeling Tired: 10 Mind-Body Steps to Fight Fatigue and Feel Your Best!* (New Harbinger), *Stop Worrying About Your Health: How to Quit Obsessing About Symptoms and Feel Better Now!* (New Harbinger), *Shy Bladder Syndrome* (New Harbinger), *Fastfacts for Human Sexuality* (Author's Choice), *1,001 Excuses: How To Get Out Of...And Away With... Almost Anything!* (Loompanics), *Quickreview Developmental Psychology* (Cliffs Notes), *Quickreview Sociology* (Cliffs Notes), *Human Sexuality: Contemporary Perspectives* (HarperCollins), *Don't Let Them Psych You Out!* (Korean Edition, Young Media), *Don't Let Them Psych You Out!* (Loompanics), and *Anxiety Disorders: A Rational-Emotive Perspective* (Macmillan).